Anonymous

Christ's Work of Reform

Anonymous

Christ's Work of Reform

ISBN/EAN: 9783337296810

Printed in Europe, USA, Canada, Australia, Japan

Cover: Foto ©Lupo / pixelio.de

More available books at **www.hansebooks.com**

A Glance at First Principles.

CHRIST'S WORK OF REFORM.

A Bible View.

BY A LAYMAN.

BOSTON:
PUBLISHED BY CROCKER & BREWSTER.
1862.

PREFACE.

In the progress which marks this age, the Christian pilgrim loves to note the footprints of his Redeemer moving on for the establishment of his kingdom. He delights to trace the advance in the arts and sciences to this source, and to connect the overturning among the nations with the declared purpose, that "He whose right it is may reign."

More especially does he delight to observe the Master's hand in the overthrow of error and the progress of religious truth. This is developed in many ways. Sabbath schools and Bible classes have opened up a new era in the religious world. Theological investigations are no longer confined to the learned divine to the same extent as in former ages. It is now by no means an uncommon thing for the secular newspapers of the day to participate in a free discussion of reformatory principles, and even to indulge in an occasional dip into theological science. In our current literature great exertions are made to popularize Christian principles.

These circumstances, among others, should be hailed with joy as indications of valuable progress. And yet these advance movements warn Christ's followers more emphatically than ever to "prove all things — hold fast that which is good" — since they are also characterized by the footprints of the great enemy, who, as an "angel of light," is seeking to palm off *his* "improvements," under the guise of religious *reform*. It is evident that the leading characteristic of much of our religious fictitious literature is not favorable to true reform, though it vauntingly claims to have accomplished this end. It aims too often to dress up human nature so as to please the carnal mind, rather than to adopt Christ's method of reform, which is, by imparting the supernatural; and when this channel is selected as a reformatory agency, we see there is a tendency to sacrifice the truth through a desire to please.

This tendency at times finds its way into the sacred desk. One of the most popular preachers of our Calvinistic communion has said that "our novels have been better reformers for the last twenty years than our pulpits." Although this comparison was made upon a broad view of all nominal Christianity, we still incline, even in that light, to place a much higher comparative value upon the efficacy of our pulpits. It must, however, be confessed that there has been for the last twenty years an apparent disposition to change and modify the good old Puritan principles of reform manifested by not a few of those who subscribe to that creed.

An inclination also prevails to uproot the old landmarks of our Calvinistic churches under the plea of "progress" and "improvements;" and in many instances, where the ancient metes and bounds are suffered to remain, they are virtually stripped of all significance by the ingenious dodge that "the substance of doctrine" is taken; while, in fact, the substance is rejected, and little is left but "the skin of truth."

This modification in doctrine and the introduction of so-called "improvements," in the old theology of the Puritan type, has presented the "new birth" in a new aspect. For the old view of a supernatural "change of heart" we have substituted a "change of purpose;" and for a will subdued to God's spiritual reign we have substituted a willingness to change the manner of life, in outward religious duties.

Sabbath schools, so hopeful for the prosperity of the church, are the first to feel the unholy influence of such superficial training; and where the young come into the church under such influences, it is not strange to find them more ready to follow the *popular religious current,* than to "try the spirits whether they are from God," or man. And it having become *popular* to unsettle foundation-principles, we often find in the same denomination those who subscribe to the same creed, yet entertain directly opposite views of practical truth. Some extol the doctrines of the Bible, while they disparage good works; others plead for a practical Christianity, while they subvert the very foundation upon which all righteous practice is built. Others there are who strive to combine a true faith in beautiful harmony with good works.

One class of religious teachers would represent the institution of slavery, as it exists in our land, as a great moral and political evil; while others treat it as of divine establishment, and lying at the "foundation of the best regulated domestic and civil institutions." One class would therefore restrict and circumscribe its limits and labor for its overthrow, while the other would "deluge the land in blood" to maintain the right to enlarge and extend its dominion. As a natural consequence, the very existence of our government is jeopardized by a most unrighteous war, which is waged against it by those who are under the most sacred obligations to devote themselves to its maintenance. Those who remain loyal and true to their sacred obligations would sacrifice their lives in the defence of that government, as a duty they owe to God and man, while those in rebellion do not hesitate to invoke the favor of God upon their efforts to subvert its very foundation.

It is, then, a priceless blessing that the fundamental principles of gospel reform are open to the comprehension of common minds, and capable of being applied by them to the common walks of life. They are revealed, not for philosophical speculations, but for practical results. They constitute a precious mine, into which common laborers may dig, and from which they may bring up the valuable treasure, and send it forth to be used as a circulating medium in the advancement of Christ's kingdom.

The times imperatively demand that every Christian citizen should investigate for himself the nature of *God's principles of righteousness*, and his method of rendering them effective, and that then he should faithfully apply them to every department of life, both by precept and by example.

The following pages are presented with a strong desire to promote such investigation. In glancing at the simple rudiments of Christian ethics as established by the Great Reformer, the appeal is made "to the law and to the testimony," in the hope that thereby something may be contributed to hasten the time when Christian principles shall become the governing principles in all departments of life, and be extended throughout the earth.

CONTENTS.

NUMBER.		PAGE
I.	CHRIST REFORMS BY UNITING THE SOUL TO HIMSELF	11
II.	THE FOUNDATION FOR UNION WITH CHRIST	25
III.	UNION WITH CHRIST IN HOLINESS A NEW CREATION	34
IV.	CHRIST'S TERMS OF UNION ADAPTED TO THE SINNER'S CONDITION	54
V.	THE WARFARE OF THOSE UNITED TO CHRIST. ITS PRINCIPLES	79
VI.	UNION WITH CHRIST IN HOLINESS THE FOUNDATION FOR GOOD WORKS	100
VII.	CHRIST'S REFORM BEARING UPON THE INSTITUTION OF SLAVERY	130
VIII.	TRUE PRINCIPLES FOR A BROAD CHURCH	167

CHRIST'S WORK OF REFORM.

I.

CHRIST REFORMS BY UNITING THE SOUL TO HIMSELF.

EVER since the revelation of the fall of man and the method of his recovery, a great diversity of views has existed relative to the nature of this method. Notwithstanding the fact, that Christ, "the true light," has made his appearance and distinctly demonstrated the method to the world, the diversity of views as to what he does for man in his work of redemption has still continued as great. That he came to reform the world, in some sense, is very generally admitted; but as to the nature and extent of that reformation, a wide disagreement in opinion exists.

Such diversity of opinion evidently does not result from any inherent obscurity in the revelation so given. Must it not, then, rather result from the character of the work itself, and from the very nature of man?

Revelation plainly teaches that Christ came, not only to reveal the will of God to man, but also to work a supernatural change in man's moral nature, by which the will of man is brought to act in harmony with the will of God thus revealed. The accomplishment of this great work was the well-defined object of his mission on earth. Regarding it in this light, the inquiry may well be raised, at the very outset, whether the high and heavenly nature of the work does not cause so many to draw back therefrom, and to seek out various devices of their own, more congenial to the proud nature of man.

Revelation, moreover, informs us that, in accomplishing his great work relative to the nature of man, "Christ was manifested to destroy the works of the devil," and that this arch deceiver is assiduously using his many devices to defeat this beneficent object. A favorite device seems to be, the construction of a system of salvation peculiar to himself, to act side by side with the true, which, from its congeniality with man's nature, shall serve to pacify the conscience, while, at the same time, it keeps the soul from Christ's salvation. In no attempt, perhaps, is man's great enemy more successful than in this.

We are now past the middle of the nineteenth century since Christ's advent; yet, though we talk of the dawn of millennial glory, though light is undeniably increasing and much progress is making towards that consummation, it may well be doubted whether mankind approach nearer each other in their estimation of this great subject. Indeed, amidst the conflicting opinions which characterize this age, so rife with man's philosophy, exalting in its system of salvation the power of man, which God's plan abases, — so studded with reformatory speculations, — it deserves serious consideration whether we do not now, if possible more than ever, need to go directly to the Great Teacher for guidance and counsel.

The diversity of opinion already noted as existing even among those who bear the Christian name, and the opposition from principalities and powers unseen, so far from causing discouragement and hinderance, should rather spur us on to serious investigation; leading us away, indeed, from all trust in systems of man's devising and merely philosophical speculations, and causing us to place ourselves at the feet of Jesus, that we may learn to comprehend the nature of that work which he came to accomplish for man, and the principles of reform which he inculcates.

In this spirit it is proposed, in the present instance, to direct attention to the more prominent characteristics of Christ's work as a Reformer, as embodied in his own declaration of principles, and illustrated with all their vivifying power in the lives and teachings of those whom he commissioned to act as instructors in his name.

It must, however, be borne in mind that we propose to examine only the more prominent characteristics as displayed in God's Word. The consideration of all that is implied in the investigation will afford, we doubt not, constant employ throughout eternity. A blessed privilege, indeed, will those enjoy, who shall so enter upon this investigation and participate in this work, as to join the innumerable multitudes of those who, throughout eternal ages, shall pay ceaseless homage before the throne of God for his gracious work of redeeming love!

We are prepared to enter upon such an examination with joyful anticipations as to the nature of Christ's work in its relations to sinful man, since we know that his mission was one of mercy, prompted by infinite love. In love was the entire work of redemption devised; and as the view of the nature of Christ's work and the manner of its accomplishment opens up to us, we shall encounter at every step a stream flowing from a spring of perennial love. At Christ's advent into our world, a multitude of the heavenly host united with the angelic messengers who announced the glad tidings in strains of exultant joy, "Glory to God in the highest, on earth peace, and good will towards man." His entire life was but a glowing manifestation of good will towards men. And yet his tender love is most conspicuously exhibited when we consider the great object of his coming.

He came to redeem the soul from thraldom to sin, to free it from the misery consequently ensuing. His very name, as declared by the heavenly herald, unfolds his one great purpose. "Thou shalt call his name JESUS; for he shall save his people from their sins." The race of man, in rebellion against the righteous government of God, and strenuously endeavoring to maintain their independence of his control, would establish an empire governed by laws of their own enactment, fortified by their own barren resources, regardless of God's rightful claim to sovereignty. Such is the assurance which the Bible gives; and the universal history of man is in accordance with it. "They are all under sin; as it is written, There is none righteous, no, not one. There is none that understandeth. There is none that seeketh after God. They are all gone out of the way; they are together become unprofitable; there is none that doeth good, no, not one." (Rom. 3 : 9-12.) This is an accurate description of the condition of the whole human family, both Jews and Gentiles, in existence at the time of the record. And yet, although the race were in this unrighteous and unreasonable revolt against the just and holy laws of God, arrayed in direct opposition to his lawful government, " God sent not his Son into the world to condemn the world, but that the world through him might be saved." (John 3 : 17.) " The Son of man is come to seek and save that which was lost." (Luke 19 : 10.) " This is a faithful saying, and worthy of all acceptation, that Christ Jesus came into the world to save sinners." (1 Tim. 1 : 17.) " In this was manifested the love of God towards us ; because that God sent his only begotten Son into the world, that we might live through him." (1 John 4 : 9.)

Christ's mission is, therefore, in a peculiar manner replete with love towards man. It aims to restore us to a state of peace and calm enjoyment, which can never be ours while we refuse to yield a devoted allegiance to the government which God would exercise over us.

As this contest, which man wages against his Heavenly Father, must, from the relative situation and capability of the parties at issue, prove a very unequal one, nothing is more especially adapted to excite an earnest interest in the mind of man than the knowledge that God's only begotten Son has appeared as Mediator ; and that for the accomplishment of this kindly office he took upon himself our nature, and dwelt as " God with us." In this God-man all our hopes now centre. Uniting, as he does, both God and man in his person, he is the better enabled to act as our Redeemer and Saviour ; he can thus represent both parties, God and man.

In his work as the Saviour of man, what does he accomplish for *the believer?* This is the question under consideration. For it is the believer only who becomes interested in, and benefited by, his work as such Saviour. The provision made by him is for the world ; and the invitations are given to whosoever will ; yet the saving benefit, whatever it may be, becomes available to us only through our faith in him as such Saviour. " He that believeth on him is not condemned ; but he that believeth not is condemned already, because he hath not believed in the name of the only begotten Son of God." (John 3 : 18.) " He that believeth shall be saved ; but he that believeth not shall be damned." (Mark 16 : 16.) " God so loved the world that he gave his only begotten Son, that whosoever believeth in him should not perish, but have everlasting life." (John 3 : 16.) " He that believeth on the Son hath everlasting life; he that believeth not the Son shall not see life, but the wrath of God abideth on him." (John 3:36.) "If ye believe not that I am he, ye shall die in your sins." (John 8:24.) All the teachings of our Saviour are of the same import. By faith only, as will be seen at every step of our examination, can we become savingly benefited by Christ's work. Faith is, indeed, so intimately connected with the salvation which he offers, that the want of it is regarded by him as the ground of condemnation.

From the holy nature of God and the unholy nature of man, taken in connection with the twofold nature of the Redeemer and all that he has done to prepare the way of reconciliation, we should naturally expect to find a great work wrought in the believer when this reconciliation takes place. Such, in fact, we ascertain to be the case. As in the person of the Redeemer God and man are united, so, when reconciliation takes place between God and the believer, the believing soul is united to Christ in a holy union; he is brought back to God, from whom he was before widely estranged, and united to him in holiness. No reconciliation can take place, unless this union with God in holiness follows as the result. It is not enough that we in mind imbibe the teachings of Christ and form purposes of obedience ; that we elect the service of God, and engage in external reform in our religious duties towards God ; that we unite with the people of God in the observance of such duties ; unless we are first united to Christ in holiness. The sinner who relies upon the righteousness of Christ for his acceptance with God, has become truly convinced of his alienation from God ; he is truly sensible of the righteousness of God in the requirements of his law ; he sees and feels that God is holy, just, and good, not only in the perfection of his every attribute, but also in the perfection of his law and government. He is painfully conscious that, while God is thus right in his requirements, he himself is utterly destitute of the righteousness required ; and he is therefore prepared to take side with God, decidedly and truthfully, in the condemnation of himself, and to make an unconditional surrender of himself to God's sovereign will and disposal. He has implicit confidence in the mercy of God which he sees displayed in the work of redemption, and yields himself unreservedly up into the Redeemer's hands.

The union of man with God depends upon a twofold condition ; the one positive, the other negative. He must become little in his own eyes before Christ can be magnified ; he must wholly renounce selfishness and self-love before he can be supplied with the holy love which comes from God; he must feel his own guilty helplessness before he will appreciate and receive divine strength for a divine life. We find the truth very clearly asserted and every where implied, that men are sinful by nature; that they have inherited from the head of their race a nature which is not only the occasion of sin, but which is itself sinful. This truth lies at the very root of our investigation, and must now be inferred, by way of premise, from the nature of Christ's work of reform, as will be seen at each advancing step. To this sin-sick race he has come as the Great Physician. Whatever, therefore, of true benefit we expect to receive from him, whatever of true interest we have in him, is connected with the Grand Healing Remedy for sin. He came "not to call the righteous, but sinners, to repentance." If we would become united to Christ in his righteousness, then must we know the truth as to our own unrighteousness. None will truly appreciate the union with him in his divine nature, unless convinced of the utter moral deficiency in their own.

To enter into holy fellowship with God, the Fountain of righteousness, and to become one with him in the disposition of the soul, is the basis of Christ's reform. But how can two such parties, God and man, the Creator and the created, be brought together? God is in heaven, and man on earth; God is perfect in holiness, man entirely unholy. There must, of necessity, be mediation; some way in which God may come to man, and man to God, and both unite. This is precisely Christ's work; and in mediating, he redeems, reconciles, and reforms; the reformation wrought by him going to the foundation of character and producing a radical spiritual change, which lays the foundation for righteousness and true holiness. Such is the endeared relation existing between the true believer and Christ, that the former is represented as being "in Christ;" and from the different modes of using this expression in Scripture, coupled with the declared experience of believers, it can only denote a union with him in his holiness; this being the essential element of a Christian, and the basis of all true reform. Men have their principles of union and their various theories of reform; but they wholly fail to accomplish the needful work. They may form a union with God in sentiment, and a reform in the purposes of the mind and in the outward life; but only He who blends the Divine and the human has the adequate power to unite the soul to God, and produce that reform which will restore that holy disposition which is lost in the nature of man by the transgression of the head of the race.

Sometimes believers are said to be "in Christ;" and in other instances Christ is said to be in them, God thus "dwelling in them," and they "dwelling in God." A union exists between the two. God and man, previously at variance and at an infinite distance from each other, are now become reconciled through the intervention of this God-man, the great Mediator. They centre in him and are united. Glorious union! The whole work of redemption rests here. "There is one God, and one mediator between God and men, the man Christ Jesus." (1 Tim. 2:5.) Glancing at the mission of our glorious Redeemer in its every relation, at all he did and all he suffered, from the manger to the cross, we find that, while its benefits were open to the participation of the world, its efficacy and real value cluster about the individual believer, who is thereby brought back to God in his union with Christ.

An exalted conception of the nature of this union is afforded us in the description given of it by our Saviour in that prayer, in which he commits his work and his redeemed ones to the Father, including not only those who were chosen to be with him, "but all that should believe in him through their word." "As thou, Father, art in me, and I in thee, that they also may be one in us; that the world may believe that thou hast sent me. And the glory which thou gavest me I have given them, that they may be one as we are one; I in them and thou in me, that they may be made perfect in one." (John 17 : 21–23.) Christ says to his disciples, "At that day ye shall know that I am in my Father, and ye in me, and I in you." (John 14 : 20.) "He that eateth my flesh and drinketh my blood" (that is, that by faith receiveth me) "dwelleth in me and I in him." (John 6 : 56.) "We know that we dwell in him and he in us, because he hath given us of his Spirit." (1 John 4 : 13.) "But of him are ye in Christ Jesus, who of God is made unto us wisdom, righteousness, sanctification, and redemption." (1 Cor. 1 : 30.) "For he made him to be sin for us, who knew no sin, that we might be *the righteousness of God in him.*" (2 Cor. 5 : 21.) "Christ in you, the hope of glory." Without multiplying quotations, the foregoing suffice to show that the believer has an inward spiritual union with Christ; a most blissful union, which will be his when all created things shall pass away — will embrace him when he lies down in the grave, and when he rises at the resurrection morn. When death overtakes him, he will "fall asleep in Christ;" and when earth's millions are called forth from their resting-places " with the voice of the archangel and the trump of God, *the dead in Christ* shall rise first."

If, then, we have any true conception of this holy union, we are prepared to unite with the apostle in the expression of our "joy in God through our Lord Jesus Christ, by whom we have now received the atonement;" since through this atonement alone have we the foundation of this blessed union.

Viewed in this aspect, the whole work of redemption centres in the atoning sacrifice of Christ. Towards this every type and shadow of the old ceremonial law pointed. Its worship, its priesthood in that worship, its sacrificial lamb, its sin-offering,—all prefigured Christ in his atonement; and the entire efficacy of the gospel depends upon Christ crucified for sin.

II.

THE FOUNDATION FOR UNION WITH CHRIST.

The foundation of the holy and endearing union existing between the Redeemer and the redeemed was laid by Christ at an infinite expense. Infinite — because it passes the comprehension of any finite mind; as it necessarily must, from the exalted nature of Him who "suffered for sins, the just for the unjust, that he might bring us to God." Every thing connected with the work of redemption is calculated to inspire faith and to render belief reasonable; yet we should approach the investigation of such a subject with reverential awe, bowing submissively before the throne of grace, and humbly submitting our wills to the guidance and control of the declared will of Him that sits thereon. This is reason's highest employ. What wonders do we approach when we would view the mystery of God manifest in the flesh for the redemption of the soul! From sufferings inconceivable we witness triumphs the most glorious emerging; from a death the most appalling springs forth a life divine and never fading.

The sufferings and death of Christ laid the foundation of, and prepared the way for, the recovery of the soul from its death in sin, bringing it thereby to life with God. He took upon himself the nature of man that he might occupy the sinner's place and suffer in his stead. His mission of infinite love ended in his suffering inconceivably, and at last dying as a substitute for sinners. "As Moses lifted up the serpent in the wilderness, even so was the Son of man lifted up, that whosoever believeth in him should not perish, but have eternal life." (John 3: 14, 15.) He was lifted up on the cross and became obedient unto death, that he might impart new life unto the believing soul. Through his death, life with God in holiness becomes the believer's inheritance. It is closed to the unbeliever because of his unbelief; but opened in all its richness and fulness to him who as a little child in faith receives it. As we are directed to Christ only for life with God, and to him in his expiatory sacrifice, and as we can become partakers of these high and holy privileges only through faith in him, our faith must rest upon God's word just as he has revealed it to us. Let us, then, go to the source of all light, and see how Christ is presented to us as our Saviour.

"Christ has now appeared to put away sin by

the sacrifice of himself." (Heb. 9:26.) "Christ our Passover is sacrificed for us." (1 Cor. 5:7.) "Christ has redeemed us from the curse of the law, being made a curse for us." (Gal. 3:13.) "Who his own self bare our sins in his own body on the tree, that we, being dead to sin, shall live unto righteousness; by whose stripes ye were healed." (1 Pet. 2:24.) "And you, who were sometimes alienated and enemies in your minds by wicked works, yet now hath he reconciled in the body of his flesh through death, to present you holy and unblamable and unreprovable in his sight." (Col. 1:21, 22.) "But he was wounded for our transgressions; he was bruised for our iniquities; the chastisement of our peace was upon him; and with his stripes we are healed." (Is. 53:5.) "If, when we were enemies, we were reconciled to God by the death of his Son, much more, being reconciled, we shall be saved by his life." (Rom. 5:10.) "The Lord hath laid on him the iniquity of us all." (Is. 53:6.) "But now the righteousness of God without the law is manifested, being witnessed by the law and the prophets; even the righteousness of God, which is by faith of Jesus Christ unto all and upon all them that believe." (Rom. 3:21, 22.) "Not as the offence, so also is the free gift. For if through the offence of one many be dead, much more the grace of God and the gift by grace, which is by one man, Jesus Christ, hath abounded unto many. And not as it was by one that sinned, so is the gift. For the judgment was by one to condemnation; but the free gift is of many offences unto justification. For if by one man's offence death reigned by one, much more they which receive abundance of grace and the gift of righteousness shall reign in life by one, Jesus Christ. Therefore, as by the offence of one, judgment came upon all men to condemnation; even so by the righteousness of one the free gift came upon all men unto justification of life. For, as by one man's disobedience many were made sinners, so by the obedience of one shall many be made righteous. Moreover, the law entered that the offence might abound. But where sin abounded grace did much more abound. That, as sin hath reigned unto death, even so might grace reign through righteousness unto eternal life by Jesus Christ our Lord." (Rom. 5: 15–21.) "In those days Judah shall be saved, and Israel shall dwell safely; and this is his name whereby he shall be called, THE LORD OUR RIGHTEOUSNESS." (Jer. 23: 6.)

These selections of Scripture are in consonance with its uniform teachings on this subject, presenting truth of such vast importance as to claim our most careful consideration. It is the central truth of revelation; to this point all other truths connected with salvation converge. It forms the basis for all substantial and enduring reform; it is the only remedy adequate to meet the malignant disease of sin in all its various forms and in its deepest and most hidden recesses.

This subject has enlisted very able discussion by theologians, who have arrived at conclusions widely different as to its grand designs as well as its various bearings; such differing conclusions being evidently very much controlled by the different views entertained of sin by them. Those who look upon sin as a mere matter of accident, or of education, or as only a disturbance in the balance of the sensibilities, and as being, in its worst aspect, of such a nature that by putting forth a strenuous determination against it — by bringing the energies of the inward will to bear upon the perverse propensities and the outward walk — they may suppress the moral evil, become exempt from it, and achieve a victory over it — such may be expected to dispense with the vital principles of this infinite sacrifice. This is, in truth, usually the case.

But those who look upon sin as a constitutional taint, fixed upon them from their birth and pervading all their faculties, — who believe that the will itself is corrupt, and that an original and inborn sinfulness runs through their entire nature,—must, if possessed of any depth of reflection, conclude that, under such circumstances, it is suicidal to turn away from a remedy so perfectly adapted to meet their condition. They can have no hope from any remedy that does not in its application offer the cure for a sinful nature, and redemption from the disposition to sin, as well as deliverance from the penalty of a violated law. The whole range of human power and human experience supplies us with nothing that can purge away the inveterate foulness wherewith our nature is stained.

It would be interesting and profitable to follow out the instructions which have been presented to enforce this truth; although it can scarcely be made more comprehensible than in the plain, simple language of Scripture previously given. When it is said, he " suffered, the just for the unjust, *that he might bring us to God;* " that it is " by his stripes *we are healed;* " that by his death he presents the believer " holy and unblamable and unreprovable in God's sight," no language can present with more distinctness its grand design. When we see its complete efficacy in taking away sin, can there be any ground for murmuring at our lot and censuring our Maker for our connection with a race so fallen? Seeing that a price of such immensity of value has been paid for the redemption of the soul from its sinful state, shall we not rather acknowledge our deep guilt, and probe to the depths of our innate depraved propensities, with all the accumulation of wicked works, and then, with all this before us, direct our attention to the Eternal Son girding himself and going forth in all the strength of his omnipotence to do battle for us against it?

As we gaze upon this wonderful sacrifice as he is presented to us in Gethsemane's garden and upon the cross, where in the agonies of the conflict he endured in his own person what it is impossible for finite minds to estimate, shall we not readily believe in his ability and willingness to subdue our inbred corruptions, and to bring us into conformity with the will of God? What mean those conflicts of soul, when, as it is recorded, " being in an agony he prayed more earnestly, and his sweat was as it were great drops of blood falling down to the ground." (Luke 22:44.) This was " the precious blood " that was " to purge the conscience from dead works to serve the living God." Shall we not believe in the power of the Eternal Spirit to apply this precious blood for the purification of our noble faculties, so that they may have life with God? The blessed Redeemer says, " Only believe, and my blood shall be applied for the cleansing of the soul, and I will present you holy and unblamable and unreprovable in the sight of God."

As we "behold the Lamb of God, offered without spot to God," extended upon the cross, what mean those piercing cries, "My God, my God, why hast thou forsaken me!" issuing from the lips of infinite purity? Although we may not comprehend the nature and extent of those soul-agonies, still the clear and vivid description which God has mercifully given to us makes it plain that this load of sin which is upon us, pressing us down with its awful weight, was borne for us by our glorious Redeemer. He was the mighty sufferer who bore it away for us. Viewing it thus, how can we refuse to acknowledge the deep guilt of our sinful state, abhorring and condemning it, and with deep contrition of soul casting our burden of wretchedness upon Him who thus offers to remove it completely from us? By this gracious substitute God's justice stands perfect and his law untarnished, though he pardons the guilty offender. But pardon is not all that we need in order to meet our condition as sinners. So far is this from being all, that, if it were possible for us to receive a full pardon for our sins without being also made holy in the reception of the same, the wants of our sinful state would not be supplied. We must partake of Christ's *righteousness in our natures* that we may become right with God and truly reconciled to him in heart, so as to enjoy true peace with him. This is offered to us in perfection in the ever-flowing founts of redemption. That image of God which was lost to us in Adam, our head, is restored to us in "the Lord our Righteousness." This is the great end accomplished in the work of redemption; and no true and lasting benefit accrues to us therefrom, if this does not accompany it. We must stand before a God of infinite perfection and holiness in righteousness other than our own, and we continually stand in need of an imputed, as well as an infused, righteousness; and the merits of Christ must be placed to our account as well as his nature laid upon our person. This only can avail with God; and this is accomplished in the union with Christ which the believer enjoys. In Christ we become sharers in his perfect righteousness, purchased by him for us through perfect obedience and by painful death; and through faith in him as our substitute we so partake of its benefits that God can deal with us as if we were deserving creatures, and receive us into holy communion with himself.

III.

UNION WITH CHRIST IN HOLINESS A NEW CREATION.

When the Redeemer had finished his mediatorial work on earth, and had "suffered as it was written of him," thus laying the foundation for a holy union between God and man, he returned to his throne in glory. He had set up a kingdom, and established its principles — " a kingdom which is to break in pieces and consume all other kingdoms, and to stand forever." (Dan. 2 : 44.) Its principles must, therefore, be thoroughly reformatory in nature and design. Its main efficacy for reform consists in its heavenly origin and the supernatural agency at work in its accomplishment. "It is not of this world;" its principles do not accord with the standard of this world; nor is it advanced by merely natural laws, but by supernatural power. The work of reform is, indeed, committed to earthen vessels, as the chosen instruments for its extension ; but the power which renders it effectual is from God.

When Christ had " showed himself alive " to his chosen apostles, after his passion, by many infallible proofs, "being seen of them forty days, and speaking of the things pertaining to the kingdom of God," he appointed them his agents for the extension of that kingdom. "And he said unto them, Thus it is written, and thus it behooved Christ to suffer, and to arise from the dead the third day; and that repentance and remission of sins should be preached in his name among all nations, beginning at Jerusalem. Go ye, therefore, into all the world, and preach the gospel to every creature. And, behold, I send the promise of the Father upon you; but tarry ye in the city of Jerusalem till ye be endued with power from on high." (Luke 24: 46, 47, 49.) "For," said he, "John truly baptized with water; but ye shall be baptized with the Holy Ghost not many days hence." (Acts 1: 5.) Christ's kingdom, therefore, is spiritual; it is set up in the heart by the power of the Holy Spirit; and its true nature is not understood, except through divine illumination. "It is expedient for you" (says the Saviour, in John 16: 7) "that I go away; for if I go not away, the Comforter will not come unto you; but if I depart, I will send him unto you." The presence of the Comforter is better, because it is his especial office to render Christ's work of reform effectual.

The basis for the recovery of the soul from

sin, and its consequent restoration to holiness, has been laid by the Redeemer; but the building upon that basis is the work of the Spirit. It is his office " to reprove the world of sin and of righteousness and of judgment;" and we are able to understand the true nature of sin, and the righteousness which God requires, only as the Spirit reveals the same unto us. Man by nature is in darkness upon this subject, having no correct perception of holiness. He must have this divine light enkindled in the soul, or perish in darkness and despair forever. " The god of this world hath blinded the eyes of them that believe not, lest the light of the glorious gospel of Christ, who is the image of God, should shine unto them." True, " the prince of this world is judged," and his dominion in the world is to be overthrown ; but it can never be achieved save by the power of the Holy Spirit, who " takes of the things of Christ and shows them unto us." Christ, the true light, has distinctly made known the will of God in the instructions which he has given; and it is in the constant and faithful application and use of these instructions that the soul is united to Christ in holiness. He has, however, provided for the redeemed something infinitely better than the mere force of these motives, or they would never taste the joys of true holiness.

This is very forcibly presented to our view by a comparison of the effect of Christ's instructions with the result produced by " the preaching of the word " on the day of Pentecost, and afterwards by his chosen ambassadors. " Never man spake like this man," (the Saviour,) in the persuasive power and constraining motives brought to bear upon the mind and conscience of man; never was the utterance of man so well adapted to sway the soul. And yet we see that a single sermon of Peter, accompanied as it was by the promised " baptism of the Holy Spirit," was more effectual in its results for the reform of the inner life than even the preaching of Him who announced those heavenly messages of love and mercy. This circumstance of itself establishes the vast importance to sinful man of Christ's method of rendering his work potent for salvation, and enables us to comprehend in some degree the immense value belonging to the mission of the Holy Spirit. When the sinner fully yields to Christ, there is a change wrought in the soul by the influence of the Spirit, infinitely above that produced by the mere force of the motives themselves which the gospel presents. The mind is, indeed, affected by these motives; but the power at work which produces the change is divine.

In this consists the crowning excellence of the

work of redemption; for without this change wrought by the Spirit, all the priceless instructions of Christ, all his sufferings, all his blood, are ineffectual for true reform.

The apostle says, "If any man be in Christ he is a new creature; old things are passed away; behold, all things are become new." (2 Cor. 5 : 17.) It is a new creation; thus conveying the idea that the original creation had become impaired and defective — so impaired and defective that it must be again performed. This, indeed, we find to be the unvarying language of Scripture. It is the peculiar office of the Spirit to convince of this deficiency, and to make the remedy for it effectual. He who endured so much agony to bring lost man back to God, assuredly knew what was requisite to make man a participator in the benefits purchased by him. The need existing he has very plainly unfolded to us. "Verily, verily, I say unto thee, Except a man be born again he cannot see the kingdom of God." Nicodemus, understanding him to speak of a new birth, (yet, as he knew nothing of the great change which must take place in man in order to restore to him the holy image of God, conceiving that he alluded to a new natural birth,) says, "How can a man be born when he is old?" Christ's reply is, "That which is born of the flesh is flesh; that which is born of the Spirit is spirit." As if he had said, "If you could be born again in the sense in which you understand it, it would profit you nothing; for that which is born of the flesh would still remain of the same species. That would never introduce you into my kingdom. To gain an entrance there, a man must be Heaven-born. He must be born of water and of the Spirit, or he cannot enter the kingdom of God." From this explicit declaration of Christ it is evident that we remain what the first creation, or birth, made us, until we are created anew, or born again; and that it is truly a new birth, since something results from the change thus experienced which was not previously in existence. Nor is it difficult to understand what must be the nature of that new quality thus introduced. As it was produced by the Holy Spirit, it must partake of the nature of that Spirit. That which is born of the Spirit resembles the Author that begat. Thus much, at least, appears plain and easy of comprehension; yet there are some things connected with it of an unsearchable nature. This the Great Teacher himself asserts. He compares it to the wind. "The wind bloweth where it listeth, and thou hearest the sound thereof, but canst not tell whence it cometh and whither it goeth; so is every one that is born of the Spirit." (John 3:

8.) The effects of the wind we can perceive; its balmy breath upon ourselves we can feel; while we cannot comprehend the manner of its operation. So of the Spirit's working: we can see the glorious effects it produces in society, and can experience its gracious influences upon our own hearts, and thus learn of its benevolent nature, although we cannot understand the manner of its operation in the mind. Happy are they who are willing to be taught by infinite wisdom! Yet what multitudes there are who reject this precious boon thus offered, and spurn it from them as if it were their deadly foe,— and for no worthier reason than because it is above and beyond their comprehension! How unjust and unreasonable! It is the very grandeur and exaltation of the work that render it mysterious. Its infinite excellence consists in its being beyond the comprehension of the natural man. We use the term "natural man" in accordance with the Scriptures, which speak of "the natural man" and "the spiritual man"— a distinction which is based upon this spiritual change; and nothing is more clearly established by their teachings than that there is a spiritual, supernatural knowledge or perception of divine things, peculiar to those united to Christ in divine life. For example: nothing other than this can be intended in 1 Cor. 2: 14. "But the natural man receiveth not the things of the Spirit of God, for they are foolishness unto him; neither can he know them, because they are spiritually discerned." To the same effect, also, are the passages in John 14 : 19 ; 17 : 3 ; Matt. 11 : 27 ; and many others.

What valid reason, then, can be furnished for rejecting this truth and treating it with ridicule or contempt, simply because of its elevated nature? Christ in infinite mercy has furnished to those who believe in him a quality of soul which is immeasurably superior to any attribute of the natural man; so much superior and so vastly different, that man can have no correct conception of its essence, but by an actual experience of its blessed reality. Shall we on that account reject it? Those who do reject it cannot with any propriety set up their own judgment as a standard by which to test the reality of such an experience in the case of those who claim to enjoy it. The apostle says, "For God, who commanded the light to shine out of darkness, hath shined into our hearts, to give *the light of the knowledge of the glory of God* in the face of Jesus Christ." (2 Cor. 4 : 6.) To the living reality of this kind of experience the Saviour has always had a faithful band of true witnesses from that time to the present; a band, too, that in numbers has greatly increased from time to time.

Now, "what if some do not believe? Shall their unbelief make the faith of God without effect" in those who do? Evidently it will shut out the unbeliever from a participation in its blessed effects, for the Spirit produces this glorious change by working faith in us, and thereby uniting us to Christ; but, happily, the precious truth remains immutable as the eternal throne — a truth which affords the only effectual means for elevating fallen humanity!

The change which is wrought in the believer, we are every where informed, is for the purpose of supplying a moral deficiency in our nature, to meet which was the great design of Christ's redemptory work. In the fall of Adam we have presented to us, as a consequence, the fall of the race of man, involving the loss of holiness, God's moral image. In Christ's redemptory work we have presented to us God's method of recovery. In the exhibition of that method and in the nature of the work accomplished in the recovery, God has displayed infinite benevolence. Why, then, should any tongue speak against it? True, it involves a humiliating view of the condition of the race, presenting, as it does, a moral defection which is entire; but, to meet it, we have presented a remedy full to completion. This glaring deficiency in our moral nature can be supplied by One who is in every way adequate to the undertaking. The Holy Spirit, in communicating himself to the believer in the new life, brings him into the most intimate and tender relations with his heavenly Father. It is a spiritual work, in which the Holy Spirit is so imparted to, and united with, the believing soul, that the latter is represented as "being made a partaker of the divine nature," as being rendered "a temple of the living God." (2 Pet. 1:4; 2 Cor. 6:26. See, also, 1 John 3:24; 4:16; John 17:21; Heb. 12:10.)

To this new source, thus opened, must we look as the fountain from which all holy affections towards God and man emanate. None but those who are thus united to Christ in the new birth possess that experience which in the Scriptures is denominated "spiritual." Others not only do not enjoy these communications of the Spirit in so high a degree as they, but in reality they possess nothing of the same nature or kind. Those holy and gracious influences of which those "in Christ" are the subjects, proceeding, as they do, so directly from the Holy Spirit, are altogether supernatural, differing widely from any lower experience, which is enjoyed by those out of Christ. No improvement or adjustment of natural qualifications or principles can ever produce them; since they differ from what is natural and from every thing experienced by natural man, not only in degree and circumstance, but also in kind. The new spiritual life, implanted in the soul when it is born of God, and the new disposition attending it, are not, however, new faculties; but a new spiritual foundation is laid in the soul, from which result holy exercises of our natural faculties; this spiritual life producing a new kind of exercise of the faculties. New faculties, in fact, we do not need. We have the faculty to love God as he requires, since we can and do love objects far inferior to him, and unworthy of our affections. We show an ability and disposition to love self supremely, when we ought to love God supremely. We, therefore, need no new faculty to enable us to love God as we ought; but we do need precisely that moral change in the soul which Christ came to accomplish, before these faculties will go out in holy affection towards God and man.*

The Holy Spirit, in his common operations upon the minds of natural men, moves, impresses, assists; or, in other words, acts in accordance with, and upon, natural principles. He may aid their reasonings upon the truths of revelation, and help them to understand its doctrines, and still not impart to them this new spiritual life. He may enable their consciences

---

* See "Edwards on the Religious Affections;" particularly Part III.

to work more actively, (a work performed upon natural principles,) and thus be of service in keeping the lower propensities of their nature in subjection to their higher faculties; and there are, undeniably, many methods by which the Spirit may act on the mind upon natural principles, assist in their development, and give free scope to their operation, without thereby producing any spiritual birth.

Whatever else, therefore, of truth we may believe connected with the work of redemption, we cannot be accepted of God unless we have that faith which unites to him in holiness. He himself says that otherwise we "cannot enter the kingdom of heaven." Could our heavenly Father have shown a more affectionate regard for our sinful race than is thus shown by Christ's work in the believer? For it is from this divine life, thus infused into the soul, that springs love of such moral excellence, so assimilated to God in its nature and so valuable in his esteem, that it constitutes the all-important qualification of the soul, the essence of all moral goodness. Without it the greatest knowledge and gifts, the most devoted attention to all outward duties the most self-denying labors, are all worthless in his esteem. (See, on this point, 1 Cor. ch. 13.) This heaven-born disposition contains within itself such Christ-like benevolence towards God and man, that "it is the fulfilling of the law." (Rom. 13 : 8–10 ; Gal. 5 : 14.)

The apostles, both directly and indirectly, teach the same truth as to the nature of Christ's work as does the Great Teacher himself. They would enforce purity of life in Christians, and they do it by pointing them to their high and holy origin. Thus: "Lie not one to another, seeing ye have put off the old man with his deeds, and have put on the new man, which is renewed in knowledge after the image of him that created him." (Col. 3 : 9, 10.) It is here explicitly stated that the new man (a term used in Scripture to designate one newly born) is created after the image of the Holy Spirit who created him. Again : "That ye put off, concerning the former conversation, the old man, which is corrupt according to the deceitful lusts, and be renewed in the spirit of your minds ; and that ye put on the new man, which after God is created in righteousness and true holiness." (Eph. 4 : 22–24.) Here "the new man" is described as one who after God's image is created in righteousness and true holiness. Language could not possibly be more explicit.

The loss of holiness in man is called, in the Bible, *death;* and its restoration, *life from the dead.* For example: "You hath he quickened, [made alive,] who were dead in trespasses and sins." (Eph. 2 : 1.) " You, being dead in your sins, hath he quickened together with Christ, having forgiven all trespasses." (Col. 2 : 13.) " When we were dead in sins, hath he quickened us together with Christ." (Eph. 2 : 5.) "This is the record, that God hath given us eternal life, and this life is in his Son. He that hath the Son [thus implanted within] hath life, and he that hath not the Son of God hath not life." (1 John 6 : 47.) " But these are written, that ye might believe that Jesus is the Christ, the Son of God; and that, believing, ye might have life through his name." (John 20 : 31.) " As the Father raiseth up the dead and quickeneth them, even so the Son quickeneth whom he will." (John 5 : 21.) " He that receiveth my word," says Christ, " and believeth on him that sent me, hath everlasting life, and shall not come into condemnation, but is passed from death unto life." (John 5 : 24.) " I am come, that ye might have life." (John 10 : 10.) " Verily, verily, I say unto you, He that believeth on me hath everlasting life." (John 6 : 47.)

From such examples we can understand what these Christians were by reason of their connection with the first Adam; they were " dead in trespasses and sins," " without holiness," God's moral image; such was their state by nature. Yet notice what the Holy Spirit made them in their union in the second Adam; they were "alive unto God," "quickened together with Christ," united in divine life "after the image of God." Christ came to impart new life, and this was accomplished in them by their spiritual regeneration; as the apostle describes it, "who hath delivered us from the power of darkness, and translated us into the kingdom of his dear Son." A glorious deliverance from darkness, and death! How blessed the translation — into the holy and spiritual kingdom of the Redeemer! Having its principles thus rooted in our hearts, they will prevail over our sinful propensities, and we shall "reign with him forever."

It is perfectly evident that these Christians had a new controlling principle introduced into their minds, which caused an interest superior to the mere changing of purpose towards Him and his government. It is also plain that this peculiar interest grew out of their new relation to God by virtue of the new birth. A spiritual spring was thus opened within, from which flowed peculiar and holy affections towards God as their Father. By it they had become his adopted and spiritual children, assimilated to him in a kindred feeling and sympathy. Listen to their expressions of attachment, and observe if they do not afford evidence perfectly in harmony with the description already given. "For as many as are led by the Spirit of God, they are the sons of God. But ye have received the spirit of adoption, whereby we cry, Abba, Father. The Spirit itself beareth witness with our spirit, that we are the children of God. And, if children, then heirs; heirs of God, and joint heirs with Christ." (Rom. 8 : 14–17.) "And, because ye are sons, God has sent forth the spirit of his Son into your hearts, crying, Abba, Father. Wherefore, thou art no more a servant, but a son ; and if a son, then an heir of God through Christ." (Gal. 4 : 6, 7.) "And, if ye be Christ's, then are ye Abraham's seed, and heirs according to the promise." (Gal. 3 : 29.) "Be ye, therefore, followers of God as dear children." "Behold what manner of love the Father hath bestowed upon us, that we should be called the sons of God. Therefore the world knoweth us not, because it knew him not. Beloved, now are we the sons of God, and it doth not yet appear what we shall be; but we know that when he shall appear, we shall be like him ; for we shall see him as he is. Every man that hath this hope in him, purifieth himself, even as he is pure." (1 John 3 : 1–3.)

With this child-like trust in God as their Father, they loved to magnify the power of God, thus displayed in bringing them into that endeared relation to himself. Can it be safe to reject this doctrine, as many do, for the very same reason which prompted them to glory in it? We see that it is a work involving power as great as they every where ascribe to it; and if we disparage the power and grace displayed in it, we in the same degree undervalue the true nature of the work. They ascribe the power and the glory to God. Their "faith did not stand in the wisdom of men, but in the power of God." With them the ground of hope and encouragement rested, not upon what man was in the dignity of his nature, but on what God was in his infinite mercy and grace; not because man could do so much to induce God to help and to prepare the way for it, but because God's compassion and love were manifested in extricating him from the degradation into which he had fallen. They had such elevated conceptions of the love of God, that they delighted to leave all with him; and to him alone did they direct sinners. They knew that if sinners would "look to the Lamb of God," his blood would prove available to wash away all their sins. Their language is, "As many as received Christ, *to them gave he power to become the sons of God*, even to them which believe on his name; which were born, not of blood, nor of the will of the flesh, nor of the will of man, but of God." (John 1:12.)

When the apostle Paul refers to his own birth to holiness, he ascribes it to the same divine power *working in him* that was at work in his natural birth. Thus: "When it pleased God, who separated me from my mother's womb, and called me by his grace, *to reveal his Son in me.*" If we peruse the history of his conversion, we there find the change ascribed to the same Almighty power. Some, who are unwilling to attribute to God the whole glory of the sinner's conversion, admit that the power of God was thus displayed in reference to the apostle, but make a distinction between his conversion and that of others, on account of the miraculous circumstances attending it. The apostle makes no such distinction. As the change wrought in the minds and hearts of all true believers is similar in its nature and effects, so he ascribes it to the same divine power in others, though not attended by the same miraculous circumstances. "The eyes of your understanding being enlightened; that ye may know what is the hope of his calling, and what the riches of the glory of his [Christ's] inheritance in the saints, and what is the exceeding greatness of his power to us-ward who believe, according to the working of his mighty power, which he wrought in Christ when he raised him from the dead." (Eph. 1 : 18–20. See, also, 2 Cor. 4 : 6.)

Here, the power of God at work, raising the sinner, " dead in sin," to life in God, is " according to the power which raised Christ from the dead." Again : " Whereof I was made a minister, according to the gift of the grace of God given unto me by the effectual working of his power." " Now, unto him that is able to do exceeding abundantly above all that we ask or think, according to the power that worketh in us, unto him be glory in the church of Jesus Christ throughout all ages." (Eph. 3 : 7, 20.)

Such is the emphasis every where placed upon the agency and " mighty power " of God at work in the hearts of his children, as well in the commencement of the new life as also in strengthening and perpetuating it. When God is thus enthroned in the affections he is worshipped and adored as Father, Son, and Holy Ghost, as he has revealed himself in the work of redemption. Divine worship and homage are given to each as truly as to the Infinite One. Each must, of necessity, receive equal honor, for each has wrought out the salvation which has its outgoing in the new disposition, and thus harmonized in the believer's experience the glorious Trinity in Divine Unity.

The children of God cannot assign their Saviour any inferior position, for from their own experience they have learned practically to " honor the Son even as they honor the Father;" and he reigns within them as their God. It is just as natural for the affections of God's children to go out to Jesus with supreme attachment as it is for the child to cleave to its earthly parents. Thus Stephen, when leaving the world under the most trying circumstances, " committed his soul to God, saying, 'Lord Jesus, receive my spirit.'" And this was but the natural manifestation of the new disposition received when he yielded his heart to him.

Happy are they who have this abiding union formed in life, that at death they may thus commend their souls to him, and be introduced to the innumerable company who unite in paying their adorations " to the Lamb that was slain" as " worthy to receive power and riches and wisdom and strength and honor and glory and blessing." Having yielded the heart and life to him on earth, they are thus prepared to unite in the willing homage paid " unto him that sitteth upon the throne, and unto the Lamb forever and ever."

IV.

CHRIST'S TERMS OF UNION ADAPTED TO THE SINNER'S CONDITION.

From the examination thus far of Christ's work of reform, we find that it raises the believer to a peculiarly exalted and interesting position. He is taken from a degraded state, indeed; but by being joined to Christ in a union which renders him a partaker of his holiness, he becomes an "heir to an inheritance incorruptible and undefiled, and that fadeth not away, reserved in heaven for us." A child of God! Can any finite mind grasp the full meaning of such a distinction? Even if we follow out to the best of our conceptions the glory of such an inheritance, we must still be content to know that "it doth not yet appear what we shall be; but we know that when our Saviour shall appear, we shall be like him." To "be like him" will open to us such a fulness of blessings as "has not entered into the heart of man to conceive."

Yet more of the sublimity and value of this work will be unfolded to our view, if we consider the terms upon which it is offered. For, great and glorious as it is, we could never hope to become, in any degree, partakers of its benefits, if, as a condition of our receiving them, we were first required to do any thing to render us worthy recipients. No such requirement, however, is laid upon us. It comes to us as a free gift; bestowed, not on account of any merit in us, but, on the contrary, because we are needy and destitute; and bestowed only upon those who truly feel their poverty. This destitution which Christ came to remedy is expressed in Scripture in a variety of forms; but, whatever the language used to represent it, the solemn truth is taught, that man is by nature destitute of righteousness with God. To such an extent, in fact, is he alienated from his Maker, that he has not the moral ability to extricate himself from his guilty and helpless condition. Although he possesses noble and godlike faculties, yet they are so vitiated towards God as to place him in a position of entire dependence upon his compassion. It becomes of the highest importance, therefore, for us to know that God has mercifully adapted his plan of salvation to our actual condition, producing this blissful union between himself and the sinner at the very point where the impotence of man is most deeply felt. Precisely there is Christ's righteousness applied to meet the sinner's destitution; from him he receives holy strength to meet the weakness that sin has occasioned, and he is *born of God into a new and divine life*.

Can it be that such riches of grace as we have contemplated are poured out so freely, and for the very purpose of meeting our abject poverty? Why, then, should such strenuous efforts be put forth to cover up a truth so plain? Why so many ways devised of reaching heaven by human strength alone? Why so many different standards erected, upon which men build their hopes for eternity, all of which are based upon the delusive expectations of lowering God's standard of righteousness to a conformity with their own?

A disposition to set aside God's standard of righteousness contributes more than any thing else to darken the mind upon this whole subject. His moral code, as given on Mount Sinai and reiterated and interpreted in Christ's Sermon on the Mount, is exceedingly plain. This furnishes the standard by which to regulate our moral exercises and acts in our relations to God and man. Can any one compare the state of his own heart as revealed in God's word with the righteousness required by the law, and remain tranquil in conscious security? Self-righteous serenity originates from a misapprehension of the law in its application. Such was the apostle's experience before his conversion. Referring to his condition at that time, he says, " I was alive without the law; " that is, he could live without Christ's righteousness when adopting his own false standard of what God required. How many there are at the present day in precisely the same condition! They feel the same ability to meet the requirements of God while they graduate their acts by their own estimation of righteousness, instead of taking God's estimate. If we would, like the apostle, avail ourselves of a righteousness which will stand the test with God, we must become sharers in the apostle's experience when he says, " When the commandment came, sin revived, and I died," and, " The commandment, which was ordained to life, I found to be unto death." (Rom. 7: 9, 10.) It was then that the law in its perfection was applied by the Spirit to his heart and conscience, and sin was beheld by him in its extent of vileness. The law, being perfectly suited to regulate the life with God and man, thus became a schoolmaster to impart instruction and convey a true knowledge of himself. Thus viewing, he saw his total want of that righteousness which is required by God — a want so deeply penetrating every faculty of his soul, that it could be fitly expressed only by the term *death*. In this view he became conscious of his weakness and helplessness. So deep-seated and all-pervading was the disease, that it needed a divine remedy. He says, "I had not known sin but by the law." In no other way could he have comprehended its exceeding sinfulness; and, although all who come to Christ do not have the same clear conviction of their entire sinfulness before God that the apostle did, still it is God's mode of imparting divine life, by convincing the sinner of his utter bondage to sin, in order that he may feel his complete dependence upon sovereign mercy. A correct knowledge of ourselves discloses the necessity of just such a remedy for sin as God has provided.

We thus see that in ourselves there is no strength for holiness. "When we were without strength, in due time Christ died for the ungodly." (Rom. 5:6.) "For what the law could not do in that it was weak through the flesh, God, sending his own Son in the likeness of sinful flesh and for sin, condemned sin in the flesh, that the righteousness of the law might be fulfilled in us, who walk not after the flesh, but after the Spirit." (Rom. 8:3, 4.) Here Christ's righteousness and power are represented as meeting the ungodliness and impotence of sinners. When they were without strength by reason of their sins, his death for sinners as their substitute prepared the way for imparting holiness to the ungodly. When by reason of sin we were unable to meet the holy requirements of the law, God in mercy sent his Son as an Almighty Saviour, whose death was a condemnation of sin, setting forth in the strongest possible light God's abhorrence of it. By this merciful arrangement the law is greatly magnified; and it was all provided to secure for the believer in Jesus this great result — *that spirit and temper of heart which the law required.*

Thus from the very depths of spiritual poverty and destitution we are invited to look up with hope and joyful confidence. Is it, indeed, true, that when sin has become a burden, and our spiritual destitution is deplored, we have unfolded to us a sure guide to a fountain of infinite righteousness? Yes; says the Saviour, " Blessed are the *poor in spirit,* for theirs is the kingdom of heaven." Poverty of spirit, through union with Jesus in divine life, introduces us into his kingdom, and gives us an inheritance in all its holy privileges as " joint heirs with him." This poverty of spirit is a destitution which is felt from a true application of God's law; and by tracing out the nature of God's requirements in the law, and the nature of the spiritual life imparted at the new birth, we are able to see how it is that Christ's righteousness, when applied to the believer, meets his natural destitution.

The Saviour, in giving a summary of the requirements of the law, has taught us very clearly its nature. He says, "Thou shalt love the Lord thy God with all thy heart and with all thy soul and with all thy mind. This is the first and great commandment. And the second is like unto it: Thou shalt love thy neighbor as thyself. On these two commandments hang all the law and the prophets." (Matt. 22:37–40.) The last sentence in effect asserts that these two commandments comprehend all the duty prescribed in the law and the prophets, and all the religion taught in them.

Although the law is thus perfect and holy in its requirements, and far-reaching and penetrating in its demands upon the heart, can any good being in God's universe properly wish to have one jot or tittle of its perfection abated? It is perfectly adapted to the relations we sustain to him as our moral Governor, and to our fellow-men as subjects of his moral government. The duty of obedience thus devolving upon us is complete, not only from the supreme authority and perfection of the Ruler, but also from the supreme excellence of the law in its adaptation to the subjects of his government. God, as a perfect and benevolent Being, could not require less. Although "the carnal mind, which is enmity against God," does not, while in its carnal, unrenewed state, love it, yet that does not release us from our obligations to love and obey it. The natural man does not love it, because of its perfection and holy nature; he "is not subject to it, neither, indeed, can be," (Rom. 8 : 7 ;) and in this settled aversion to God and his holy law lies the groundwork of man's alienation. At precisely this point the divergence begins, which manifests itself in the most highly-cultivated self-righteousness, and in the lowest degradation and vice.

While this is clearly man's natural state, love of the law is one of the most precious fruits of the new birth. Those who partake of Christ's righteousness in the new life rejoice exceedingly to hear their Saviour say, "Think not that I am come to destroy the law or the prophets ; I am not come to destroy, but to fulfil." Knowing and deeply feeling that " they that are in the flesh cannot please God," they rejoice that Christ has opened a way in which they can become spiritual and holy, and thus " delight in the law of God " because of its holiness. " Christ is the end of the law for righteousness to every one that believeth." (Rom. 10 : 4.) The intent and end of the law are fulfilled and perfected in Christ's work. He complied with it in all its perfection in his life on earth ; and it is delightful to trace his footsteps as he went about doing good, uttering his messages of mercy, and instructing all in the means of a holy life. Still we do not know the true excellence of its fulfilment until we look upon him in faith as "the Lamb of God that takes away our sins," and become united to him in the new life. It is only as the great atoning sacrifice that his righteousness becomes available to us; for "he suffered for sins, the just for the unjust, that he might bring us to God." (1 Pet. 3:18.) "He was made to be sin for us, who knew no sin, that we might *be made the righteousness of God in him.*" (2 Cor. 5:21.)

Here he becomes "the end of the law to every one that believeth." The reception of him into the heart accomplishes the end or object proposed in the law, namely, "justification that is of God." "We are accepted as righteous in his sight only for the righteousness of Christ," and are owned by him as obedient children, and adopted as such. And those adopted as children are made truly such. "God hath sent forth the spirit of his Son into their hearts, crying, Abba, Father." Their obedience is therefore acceptable, because the love that prompts it is a legitimate outgoing of "an heir of God through Christ." It is that kind of love which is "the fulfilling of the law." "The fruit of the Spirit is love, joy, peace, long-suffering, goodness, faith, meekness, temperance; against such there is no law." (Gal. 5:22, 23.) These holy affections, and the conduct resulting from them as the fruit of the Spirit's working in the new nature, are what the law requires, and therefore are not condemned by it. "The fruit of the Spirit is in all goodness and righteousness and truth." (Eph. 5:9.)

We learn the superiority of the love which is the fruit of the new relation over natural affection, from the terms of discipleship enjoined by the Saviour. "If any man come to me, and hate not his father, and mother, and wife, and children, and brethren, and sisters, yea, and his own life also, he cannot be my disciple." (Luke 14:26.) No words could more vividly express the deep feelings of abnegation of self with which we are to approach Christ, and which are to characterize our relations as his disciples. All the endeared objects of our natural affections are to be set aside and disregarded, if the soul would be united to Jesus. He must be the chief object of desire, and upon him the affections must centre. When the Spirit enters the soul and takes up its abode therein, he casts down all these idols, and fixes the affections upon Jesus as supreme. When Christ is truly enthroned in the heart, the change thereby wrought is of such a holy nature, and the love which springs from it, and is manifested towards Christ and holy objects, is so much superior to merely natural affection, that the latter is, in comparison with the former, as if it were hatred.

The same principle is inculcated by our Saviour when he teaches us to "love our enemies." This is not a natural disposition of the heart; and we do not possess it in its true spirit until we have learned it in this spiritual relation to Christ. By imbibing Christ's principles in our minds we may train ourselves to act kindly towards them, and even to exercise a naturally humane feeling towards them; but the feeling of holy compassion towards them we cannot know until we partake with Christ in holy love of the precious fruits of righteousness received from him. By participating with him in this love we experience the exceeding excellence of his work of redemption. This we can never compass in its vast extent only as we share with him in that love, which led him from the bliss of heaven to his earthly sufferings for the well-being of his enemies and their advancement to this state of holiness. It was "when we were enemies we were reconciled to God by the death of his Son."

Thus, in every view we take of Christ's work, and the terms in which it is applied, we find that it is perfectly adapted to the wants of sinners. In their ignorance he is "made unto them wisdom;" to their darkened minds he is "the sun of righteousness." He unites them, though allied to a sinful race, and inheriting a depraved nature, to God in holiness, and gives them an inheritance with his children. Though they are dead in sin, because dead to holiness, he applies to them his own righteousness, and imparts life divine. Though they are utterly impotent for holy exercises, his strength is perfected in their weakness. True self-knowledge, then, becomes exceedingly important; since his righteousness is applied to them in their true condition, and not in what they may erroneously fancy to be such.

It was a wise remark of one of the old New England divines, "Tell me what a man thinks of the natural condition of the race, and I will tell you the whole of his theology." One's views of this condition must of necessity have an important bearing upon the benefits of redemption. The changes of opinion transpiring in the theological world are bringing this question up for fresh investigation. The different views entertained of the native character of man mark the distinction between those who style themselves "the progressives" and "the conservatives;" whose views on this subject give shape to their reformatory principles in religion and morals.

It is claimed by many that great improvements have been made in theological science, from a better knowledge of man's nature and a fuller understanding of the mind now existing, compared with any previous age. However that may be, it is evident that the theorizing on this subject vitally affects the views taken of the nature of Christ's work, in its application for spiritual reform. True reconciliation and filial obedience can come only through the mediation of Christ. There is no other name given under heaven that can accomplish it. He only can balance and adjust these depraved faculties, and restore them to purity and holiness, so that they can move on in harmony with God and his law.

Christ in his method of reform lays the axe at the root of the tree. He would purify the stream by cleansing the fountain. He deals with man as having a corrupt and sinful nature, defiled in all its faculties; and he would give a right direction and exercise to them by imparting help where it is needed. He makes man's volitions and acts right with God, by purifying the source whence they issue ; and our wills and purposes are right with God only as he "works in us to will and to do; " the faculties of the soul being rightly exercised towards him only as we are united to Christ as closely " as the branch is united to the vine." Thus, and thus only, do we receive power to become the sons of God; and we are "born, not of blood, nor of the will of the flesh, nor of the will of man, but of God." (John 1:12, 13.) Christ's work is not merely to give to the faculties a *higher aim and purpose* by the persuasions of his truth; but it is by the power of the Spirit working with the truth as an instrument to give a new divine life to the soul, so that every faculty may be rightly developed in its relation to God and man. We may be convinced that we ought to live for the glory of God, and from that conviction form the purpose to do it; but a far deeper work is necessary, before that purpose will be carried out to his acceptance.

We are well aware that we do not treat this subject according to the method of modern improvements in theological science. We are no theologian; we make no pretension to theological skill; but often, when listening to discourses upon salvation based upon the power inherent in man's nature for the production of holiness, we have felt like exclaiming, "Ye have taken away my Lord, and I know not where ye have laid him!" Not that he had no place assigned him; but he had not his *true* position. And although they mete out to him a high tribute of praise, yet it is all as "sounding brass or a tinkling cymbal" when we find that the position they assign him is *only subordinate*. Not so discoursed those holy ambassadors, faithful and true, whose teachings we are considering. They love to dwell upon the surpassing greatness of Christ's power " to us-ward who believe." In their estimation the work was so great and of such a nature, that nothing less than almighty power could accomplish it. But their Saviour was almighty; the promised Comforter, from whom they received their sanctifying power, was almighty; and their faith rested not in the wisdom of man, but in the power of God. They entertained no fears, in thus magnifying " Christ as the power of God and the wisdom of God unto salvation," that they should detract, in the slightest degree, from the responsibility of man in his free agency. Such fears are the offspring of unbelief, and do not result from faith in the power of God.

True, we do not hear them discourse upon man's free agency; and certainly they had no philosophy respecting it which recognized the existence of any faculty in man as independent of God. They certainly had a true knowledge of man in his relations to God, and they recognized in him high and exalted faculties, capable of rendering, *if so disposed*, true obedience, and they therefore held him accountable for the right exercise of these faculties; but they did not fear to deal with his moral defection and impotence on their true ground. They surely had no theory of man's nature and free agency which deterred them from speaking of his moral impotence, and of almighty strength as ready to meet it, which was to be made applicable through that very free agency; and they well knew that they addressed those who were perfectly conscious that they acted freely and voluntarily in accepting or rejecting proffered help. They acted upon the principle that this consciousness pervaded every rational mind, and that their hearers knew themselves to act just as freely in accepting God's terms of reconciliation to himself, as they did in their rebellion against him. In all their teachings they assume this as a truth so self-evident, so inwrought into the very fibre of man's intellectual being, that no labor was necessary to demonstrate it.

They came, therefore, with their proclamation of mercy, addressing men as in rebellion against their rightful moral Governor, holding forth his terms of pardon and reconciliation, and pointing to Christ as their only Mediator and Saviour; and they were full of hope and zeal, because the power to make his work effectual was of God. They knew that those to whom pardon was so freely proffered were as free in "working out their own salvation by God's working in them to will and to do," as they were in working out their own destruction by persisting in their unnatural revolt. Cavillers would be found, they were well aware, (for they exist in all times and places;) but they could not alter the terms, nor lower the standard, to suit the capacities or depravities of the rebels. Had they attempted it, destruction to the souls for whose salvation they were laboring must inevitably have ensued.

To all appearance they were led on in their exertions for the good of man by a love of souls, kindled in them when they lay helplessly submissive at the foot of the Cross. They knew well its efficacy to remove sin. They knew that the power which wrought in them was God's power, and in that lay their chief joy and glory. They knew, moreover, that in receiving it into the soul and exhaling it in holy union with Christ they were acting most freely; it was sweet to know and to feel that creative power was thus working within them, turning their affections from self and its endeared objects to God and holiness; their own choice and will having free scope and play, though moved by the Spirit, in these exercises. They never paused to inquire, "How can these things be?" nor did they rest in their labors of love to explain how God's agency and man's agency are combined in this holy union with Christ. They were content to leave it, where God would have them, among the mysteries of his work of redemption; and a happy day will it be for Christ's kingdom when all who are acting as his ambassadors shall follow their example.

It is not necessary that we understand why sin corrupted the race, so that in our nature there is a universal disposition to sin, or how God's power and the freedom of man's volitions combine in applying the work of redemption for its cure; yet it is necessary that we understand the moral destitution of our nature and our own inability to apply the remedy, since by it Christ's salvation becomes truly appreciated.

The very freeness of the gospel invitations implies a moral destitution which Christ's power only can supply. It is refreshing to listen to these cheering invitations, not only because they are so freely offered, but also on account of the nature of the supply furnished. Let us look at a few examples. " In the last day, that great day of the feast, Jesus stood and cried, If any man thirst, let him come unto me and drink." (John 7: 37.) " Come unto me, all ye that labor and are heavy-laden, and I will give you rest. Take my yoke upon you, and learn of me; for I am meek and lowly in heart; and ye shall find rest unto your souls." (Matt. 11: 28, 29.) " The Spirit and the bride say, Come. And let him that heareth say, Come. And let him that is athirst come. And whosoever will, let him take of the water of life freely." (Rev. 22:

17.) "Whosoever drinketh of the water that I shall give him shall never thirst; but the water that I shall give him shall be in him a well of water springing up into everlasting life." (John 4:14.) "And Jesus said unto them, I am the bread of life; he that cometh to me shall never hunger; and he that believeth in me shall never thirst." (John 6:35.)

Here the new disposition which the Spirit produces in the soul in the new creation is called "the water of life" and "the bread of life," because it is the soul's true sustenance and nourishment. Holiness is the only soul-satisfying good. It is that upon which the soul in its original state was made to feed. In its revolt from God the soul feeds upon the husks which it picks up by its own resources, and famishes for want of its natural aliment. "The bread of God is he which cometh down from heaven and giveth life unto the world;" and the soul can never experience true peace and happiness until it is brought back to God, and is exercised in harmony with him in his holiness. Language could not more vividly portray the freeness with which the heavenly manna is offered. God not only thus freely invites, but he takes his place with us, and in the most affectionate language reasons and expostulates with us. "Why do ye spend your money for that which is not bread, and your labor for that which satisfieth not?" In the offer of this heavenly gift, our minds are thus brought to act in relation to it; "life and death are thus set before us," and we are to choose between them. All who hear these heavenly invitations exercise their free choice by accepting or rejecting them.

All are apparently pleased with this condescension, and the winning manner in which the Saviour comes in his invitations; but yet, how is the love so vividly manifested abused! How many listen, and applaud the *manner*, but utterly *reject* the gift! Nor is this confined to the openly immoral and rebellious alone; but its spirit is deeply seated in the human soul, and manifests itself in every aspect in which we regard Christ's mediatorial work, and in the manner in which it is treated. It is not because men have no desire that their religious wants should be met. A strong desire towards this is often seen in the heathen world, as well as under the light of the gospel. In the latter it is displayed in the various forms of man-religion. Men do not object to the gospel system of salvation, if it can be adjusted according to their cherished dispositions.

But, evidently, the benefits of redemption cannot be received on such terms. For herein lies the spirit of rebellion, and unless this point is yielded, there can be no true reconciliation. This dissatisfaction towards God must be cured, and this cannot be done by dictating terms to him. How many spurn from them " the water of life" pouring in all its freeness, because of its divine nature and of the divine power from which it flows! What though it be offered as a free gift, purchased at an infinite sacrifice? What though it be a new fountain of spiritual life, which "shall be in them a well of water springing up into everlasting life"? What though from this fountain issue those holy affections which control and regulate all the faculties in harmony with God and his law? Despite all this, if all these riches of grace flow out to supply a conscious destitution which they are morally unable to supply, the rebellious spirit murmurs, "It is not in accordance with the laws of free agency." And, though such be the utterance of a rebellious spirit, it claims deference, and often receives it from those who would win souls to Christ — even Christ's ambassadors being not infrequently found dallying with it.

Human power has been taxed to its utmost ability to devise a scheme by which gospel principles can be so adjusted as to leave this strong citadel undisturbed. Human learning and philosophy are summoned to aid in this adjustment. For this purpose the mind is dissected, and all its faculties minutely analyzed, and their relative position to each other accurately defined. But yet, has the end aimed at been reached? There is no lack of learned speculations and of confident theories which put forth pretentious claims to such a result; yet upon investigation they are all found to excite only hopes which delude for a time, and are sure to end in bitter disappointment.

The grand defect of all such philosophical adjustments upon natural principles is, that they do not deal truly with man's moral nature. All theories based upon "the power of free will," or "the power of a contrary choice," — "the power to control and change the soul's own unwillingness and disinclination," — about which we hear so much from a class of theologians and reformers — can never meet the moral wants of man, from the fact that they deal with an *assumed*, and not with his *real*, condition. They may truly present the relation which the natural faculties sustain to each other, but they give an entirely false view of the relation which the whole sustain to God. How much precious truth is thus lost, as to any saving efficacy, because it is not applied to the seat of the disease! Under such an application it can only operate as a palliative; it can never restore; and labors and toils, however valuable in themselves, that are based upon this *assumed* condition, are as destitute of holy vitality as is a skilfully-adjusted skeleton of dry bones. The saving efficacy of Christ's reform is not adapted to the existing moral power in man, but to his want of it; and to such as receive Christ's salvation he " gives power to become the sons of God." When this is accomplished the faculties are not only regulated in harmony with each other, but all are reconciled to God and brought into harmonious accord with his law.

The Saviour says, " Ye will not come unto me, that ye may have life; " and how true it is that sinners are willing to do every thing else, however self-denying, rather than to come as beggars for the very thing they need, which Christ came to impart—life, spiritual, divine, eternal ! Christ must have the entire control in order to work effectually for salvation. Many are very glad to avail themselves of his *assistance* to adorn their *self*-righteousness, but will not submit wholly to *his* righteousness. But when his righteousness is inwrought into the soul, there must be an unconditional surrender to him. Blessed privilege! Who that know themselves, that have a correct knowledge of their unrighteous disposition by nature, and have learned by experience the delightful contrast which the new disposition affords, will ever complain that they are not free, because in the surrender Christ does for them what they deeply feel they have not the moral power to do for themselves? On the contrary, they magnify "the power of God and the wisdom of God;" not only because it comes to them as a free gift, but because they are free in the exercise of every volition in its reception; and, most of all, because their holy affections emanate from a new spiritual fountain, which is the water of life to their thirsty souls. Our old affections will cleave to earth and earthly good, and retain their obstinate and undisputed hold, till we yield to Him whose right it is to reign. He it is that presents these new objects and new affections, which satisfy the spiritual wants of the soul.

Do any object because Christ does so much in applying his work of redemption, and say that they are not free and accountable, if thus dependent? We leave them to settle the controversy with Him to whom alone they are accountable. They do not pretend that they are not free in their objections, and in thus rejecting his work; and we never heard of one that professed to have experienced its transforming power that did not rejoice in his freedom. In each case, then, there is freedom, in choice and action; though one is the freedom of a rebel, the other that of a loyal subject.

But it is said, that, although we are thus free

in submission and in union with Christ in the divine life, yet this doctrine of entire dependence upon the good pleasure of Christ for regenerating power has a tendency to discourage the sinner, and that he must in some way be relieved of that discouragement, that he may make an effort for, and thus attain, salvation. This objection shows very conclusively the relative position in which Christ is held. Entire dependence upon Christ calculated to discourage effort! Upon what, then, can we rely, which is more hopeful? To what other source can we look for needed help? To what source do Christ's inspired ambassadors direct for hope and encouragement? While they encourage effort in the use of all of God's appointed means, do they afford the slightest encouragement to expect saving efficacy from any source but Christ? No, never. In all their appeals they point for encouragement, not to man's moral strength for righteousness, but to his guilty helplessness, and to the Infinite Fountain of righteousness made applicable by the Spirit's power.

This is God's philosophy; and all attempts to modify or improve upon it will only result, at best, in an improved form of self-righteousness.

V.

THE WARFARE OF THOSE UNITED TO CHRIST. ITS PRINCIPLES.

How are we to understand the expression, used as descriptive of a person united to Christ, "Old things are passed away, and behold all things are become new"? To what extent is he a new creature? How is he exhibited in his inward experience and outward life?

We have seen that he is in a new state with God. Previously to his union with Christ he was under condemnation by God's law; afterwards he is "justified freely by his grace, through the redemption which is in Christ." He was afar off, at an infinite distance, in his moral nature; he is now "made nigh by the blood of Christ." He was a stranger and foreigner; he is now "a fellow-citizen with the saints, and of the household of God." He was "by nature a child of wrath;" he is now by grace "a child of God."

Though this is his happy state in his relation to God, and although by virtue of his union with Christ he becomes "a partaker of the divine nature," and is "created in righteousness and true holiness," yet his position is attended with peculiar trials and temptations. It is of importance, therefore, that we understand what the Bible declares the inward experience of a Christian to be. In the light of its declarations we may see the development of the divine life in its internal operations, and the principles which regulate such development. We can, moreover, find therein presented such principles as will be safe guides to those who hope that they are the children of God. If their hopes rest upon a scriptural foundation, they will not be satisfied merely with a hope that they are his children, but their desire and purpose will be, to prove themselves *obedient* children. As he who has called them is holy, they would resemble him in the exercise of holiness in all the relations of life. Having in our investigations hitherto looked to the source whence springs the water of life, it cannot prove unprofitable to trace the stream as its flows onward, widening and deepening in its course till it ends in eternal glory. Although we may be unable, in this connection, to trace its windings as manifested in all the details of the different graces of spiritual life, we shall endeavor to fasten upon general principles, which shall serve as landmarks to guide us on our way.

We have seen that those who are united to Christ have received from him, by virtue of that union, a true love of holiness as exhibited in the divine character and divine government. In an honest surrender of the heart to God, there is more than a passive acquiescence in his sovereign reign; *Christians love to have him reign.* In no respect do they more truly rejoice, than that they are at the disposal of his sovereign will. Having committed their souls to Jesus, he has taken up his reign within them as king. At his feet they love to sit and receive from him instruction for holy living, beginning now, for the first time, to comprehend the nature of true obedience; and, as the crown of all, they have truly learned, that in Christ only is there righteousness with God. They have received him as the " Lord their Righteousness; " a foretaste of what will eventuate therefrom they feel springing up within as " water of life " to a thirsty soul. Such a view of the new life within is believed to be warranted by the truth of revelation, and applicable to all who are truly united to Christ.

Although from their very nature a marked difference must exist between the exercise of love for God and holiness and those affections which spring from self and terminate in it, many true disciples are, nevertheless, greatly perplexed to decide whether they are united to Christ or not. Such perplexity arises partly from the fact, that true love towards God is oftentimes in its commencement quite weak; and of God's children in general it may be said, that they are in truth but children in divine knowledge and the divine life. The believer in Jesus, however, may have the consolation of knowing, that if there be a true filial trust in Christ for righteousness, so as to become a partaker of it, although the new love be feeble, "he will not break the bruised reed, nor quench the smoking flax." If there be but a spark of divine life, he will give it strength to overcome its opposing obstacles, by a steadfast continuance of that trust in him. To the nature of the opposition which is antagonist to the new life within, and the principles by which the warfare is successfully carried on, we propose to direct inquiry.

From our knowledge of the manner in which those in Christ became such, we can the more readily understand somewhat of the significance of those phrases which so much abound in the Epistles; as, "the old man," in contrast with "the new man," and "the flesh," in contrast with "the Spirit," used in depicting the Christian's inner life. In addressing Christians, the apostle speaks of "the old man which is corrupt" and must be "put off," and of "the new man, which is renewed after the image of him who created" them, to be "put on." "The flesh lusteth against the Spirit, and the Spirit against the flesh: and these are contrary the one to the other; so that ye cannot do the things that ye would." (Gal. 5 : 17.) From many similar descriptions of a contest and conflict in Christian experience, we may comprehend, in some degree, the nature of the Christian warfare. It is not a contest between the higher and the lower propensities of our sinful nature, or between our natural conscience and our depraved inclinations, or between selfish principles of any kind, for the subjugation of some that others may reign. Such conflicts do, indeed, take place within the natural man, and they are often, under the light of the gospel, severe and prolonged. On this account many seem to have accustomed themselves to regard the Christian warfare as of such a nature — a fatal mistake, inasmuch as it has its origin in a misconception of the reform which Christ at the new birth works in the soul. From a limited comprehension of man's depravity, and an erroneous view of his moral powers and natural wants, they think so to use Christ's salvation as to build up a righteousness which shall meet God's approval, in the absence of that radical change which our investigation discloses as the foundation of all moral excellence with him.

When those who labor thus in the Christian warfare apply to it the same truth as is applicable to the true, which is often the case, its influence may serve to beautify and adorn their self-righteousness, rendering them better citizens in the relations of life; but their righteousness can never rise higher than an *imitation* of that furnished by " the Lord our Righteousness."

And upon a comparison with the true, it will be found to be miserably defective, and all those hopes which are built upon it must be swept away when they are most needed. No, the Christian warfare is far higher in its nature and results than a mere contest between any of the dispositions at work in the natural man. Selfishness, in all its unholy working, going to make up a body of sinful propensities, wars against Christ-like benevolence, or holy love — a principle implanted in the soul when it is born of God. Such a contest furnishes us with clearer conceptions of the true nature of sin, and our own inability to arrest the downward tendency of our depraved inclinations. True love of holiness, and a burning hatred of sin, may exist within us; we may purpose to live holy, and to avoid all known sin. This the Christian will do. Still, the tendency of our depraved inclinations is opposed to holiness; and this opposition develops itself yet more distinctly as the Christian advances in the divine life.

To enable us to understand the truth in this connection, let us refer to the experience of the apostle Paul, furnished by himself many years after he had commenced the Christian life. Adverting to the law as God's standard of righteousness, he says, "For we know that the law is spiritual; but I am carnal, sold under sin. I know that in me (that is, in my flesh) there dwelleth no good thing: for to will is present with me; but how to perform that which is good I find not. I find a law, that, when I would do good, evil is present with me. For I delight in the law of God after the inward man; but I see another law in my members, warring against the law of my mind, and bringing me into captivity to the law of sin which is in my members. O wretched man that I am! Who shall deliver me from the body of this death? I thank God, through Jesus Christ our Lord." (Rom. 7 : 14–25.) Now, how could this holy apostle take to himself the blame of so much vileness and such exceeding turpitude as are here expressed? How could it be said of him who "fought the good fight," that he was sold under sin; that there dwelt in him (in his flesh) no good thing; and that he was so wretched in view of the mass of corruption from which he could not deliver himself, that he was led to cry out in his anxious helplessness, lest he should be overwhelmed?

These utterances came from one who saw the spirituality of the law in a high degree; who saw it set off in a clear light against his own sinful nature, presenting in contrast a picture fearfully dark. What, however, was the object he had in view, when he thus presented the true nature of his own sinful propensities? Was it not for the purpose of showing, that in himself he had not the power to meet the holy demands of the law? He could ever say he had true delight in it; he had already drunk deep at the fountain of spiritual life; but still he found, when sounding the depths of his depraved and still unsanctified nature, such strength in its corrupt workings, that he cried out, as if in the agony of utter destitution and helplessness, "Who shall deliver me from the body of this death?" When he looked at his own resources for perpetuating the divine life, he found the same trouble inherent which he encountered when he first saw his complete destitution of it. There was now no goodness in the flesh, as contrasted with the new and spiritual life. He could will — that was present; but how to turn the affections of the soul towards God, with all the constancy of outgoing that the law required — there was the difficulty. He might propose to live holy and to be holy, as God is holy, (as, indeed, he did;) but there still remained a body of death, from which no life-giving power could spring.

And yet this view was not presented by him in despondency. On the contrary, it was as far from it as light is from darkness. The conflict was in reality a bitter one, the struggle severe; but, thanks be to God! it was a most triumphant one in its issue. "Through Jesus Christ our Lord" victory is certain. "We are more than conquerors through him that loved us;" and the outpouring of holy love is none the less sweet because it comes so freely from "him that loved us." "There is no condemnation to them which are in Christ Jesus, who walk not after the flesh, but after the Spirit." Cleaving to him by faith, and in holy union with him in spiritual life, "the law of the spirit of life in Christ Jesus hath made us free from the law of sin and death." (Rom. 8 : 1, 2.) Riches of grace thus abounding are more precious, as they flow through such appreciated depths of poverty in ourselves. As poverty of spirit is the passport to an entrance into Christ's kingdom, so it is a passport for the reception of the continued supplies of abounding grace, which are so necessary to feed the flame of divine life. The consciousness of our extreme poverty acts as a constant stimulus to induce us to apply to the Infinite Fountain of riches of grace; and, as we drink of the water of life, we are urged on to the conflict with our unholy propensities by reason of the loathing and abhorrence which we feel for them.

The apostle's view of himself, just under consideration, prompted him to break forth in expressions of triumphant confidence, as in Rom. 8 : 37–39. "In all these things we are more than conquerors, through him that loved us. For I am persuaded, that neither death, nor life, nor angels, nor principalities, nor powers, nor things present, nor things to come, nor height, nor depth, nor any other creature, shall be able to separate us from the love of God which is in Christ Jesus our Lord." Would we know the holy love, joy, peace, security, with all their attendant blessings, resulting from the intimate bond of union between Christ and his redeemed, and illustrated in exclamations like the foregoing, we must attain that delightful vantage-ground by the same valley of humiliation and self-abasement before God through which the apostle passed ; the same feeling of our utter inability for righteousness with God must be ours, accompanied with the same inspiring faith in the righteousness of Christ to meet that deficiency. No new road leads to holiness; there is no new way wherein "to walk with God." Faith in Christ for "wisdom, righteousness, sanctification, and complete redemption," is the only band that can strengthen the cords which unite us to God in holiness. New schemes have been devised and new theories presented in abundance, as opening a better and improved way, which may allure and captivate by the temporary peace which they afford; but they cannot furnish the soul-satisfying tranquillity imparted by the Holy Comforter, nor can any possible substitute meet the wants of the human soul.

We have heretofore seen that Christ came to our rescue by reason of our entire destitution of holiness, and at precisely the time when such destitution was deeply felt, and we trusted in him alone for righteousness and acceptance. We now perceive that, being made " alive unto God " through faith in Christ, and being " justified freely by his grace," " the just shall live by faith; " so that the same principles, which were in operation for the introduction of the divine life into the soul, continue in operation for its perpetuation and increase. Distrust in our own righteousness is a universal characteristic of the Christian warfare; for Christians have learned by sad experience that there is abundant ground for such distrust. They have seen themselves " dead in sin," without hope in themselves, because without God; and every step which they have taken since they began to walk in "newness of life" has increased the evidence of their sinful nature to such an extent that the feeling has become inwrought in them, "that we are not sufficient of ourselves to think any thing as of ourselves, but our sufficiency is of God." (2 Cor. 3 : 5.)

Having learned by experience, that Christ is the author of all right exercises towards God, the desires centre in him as the supplication goes up, "Search me, O God, and know my heart; try me, and know my thoughts; and see if there be any wicked way in me, and lead me in the way everlasting." (Ps. 139 : 23, 24.) God only can know the deep depravity and the evil working of the heart, as it is "deceitful above all things and desperately wicked," (Jer. 17 : 9;) and the Holy Spirit only can give us a true sense of its wickedness, purify and cleanse it from its defilement, and turn its affections heavenward to God and holiness. Christian experience teaches that simply regulating one's volitions and acts on natural principles is not sufficient. As sin is seen in its true light, the Christian is led to probe the depths whence proceed his unholy exercises, confessing his vileness, and supplicating deliverance. The feeling of his heart is, "Behold, I was shapen in iniquity, and in sin did my mother conceive me. Behold, thou desirest truth in the inward parts, and in the hidden parts thou shalt make me to know wisdom. Create in me a clean heart, O God, and renew a right spirit within me." (Ps. 51.) With the believer, therefore, the fact " that we are by nature children of wrath," is not simply a matter of speculation, but one of great practical importance; for he has learned the utility of knowing the extent of the malady that the proper medicament may be applied.

The soul which is illuminated by the Divine Comforter, needs no labored argument to prove that the constant disposition of the natural heart is to turn away from God and holiness, and to cling to inferior objects. It knows this from its own bitter experience. No truth is more firmly fixed than this. The Christian knows and feels that without Christ's gracious help his affections as truly go out after unworthy objects, thus turning away from holiness, as the stream follows in its course its natural channel. As constantly as he is conscious of the corrupt workings of the old nature, he recognizes the absolute necessity of grace to help from the Author of life in the new nature. His blood it is that " cleanseth from all sin ; " and by resting in him alone, he more and more " dies unto sin and lives unto righteousness."

In the contest waged between sin and holiness, the grace and power of the Redeemer are more magnified, and our own weakness rendered more apparent, if we contemplate another party to the struggle. The apostle says, "We wrestle not against flesh and blood, but against principalities, against powers, against the rulers of the darkness of this world." The Christian has, therefore, to contend, not only with his own sinful nature, still unsanctified, but also against the wiles of a deceitful and powerful enemy outside of himself. Every scriptural representation establishes the fact that this enemy is exceedingly powerful in his influence upon the human mind. He is a usurper, having obtained his strong hold on this world in consequence of his success in drawing off our first parents from their allegiance to God — a hold so strong, in fact, that nought but the power of the Redeemer can overthrow it. This the arch enemy well understands. The first announcement of a Saviour refers to the might of this usurper: "The seed of the woman shall bruise the serpent's head" — declaring the doom of the original instigator to sin at the same time that it brings the first dawn of hope to the transgressor by offering a remedy for sin. Ever since that announcement we find the Bible holding this instigator forth as the great enemy of the Redeemer's reign, as being constantly at work to prevent its progress in the world. And with reason is he so; for every step in its advance is aimed directly at his overthrow. Hence his most artful stratagems are employed to avert it. Christians are instructed by the apostle to expect that his power in deceiving will be exerted to this end. He bids them not to marvel when they notice the efforts of false teachers to turn the mind " from the simplicity that is in Christ;" for, as the serpent beguiled Eve through his subtlety, they must expect that he would make use of the same means in order to corrupt their views of truth, and thus to draw them away from the plain teachings of Christ. They need not, therefore, wonder that such false teachers claim to be true; for " Satan himself is transformed into an angel of light." (2 Cor. 11 : 4, 14.) In no relation towards man is he more destructive than in this. To darken the mind and divert it from the true nature of Christ's work are prominent objects with this deceiver. His efforts in this direction meet with the most success, because he is then working with the inclinations of the natural heart. Christ's reign in the soul is established and perpetuated (as we have seen) by the subjugation of fallen self-love, or selfishness, to holy love, or Christ-like benevolence — a work which the power of the Spirit can alone accomplish; while all of Satan's efforts run in the same current with human inclinations, and, being congenial to man, are too often crowned with success in the promotion of false views of the religion of Christ.

As he led Eve astray by falsely assuring her that she should not die if she disobeyed, so now he would lead the race, dead in sin by reason of Eve's disobedience, astray by the assurance that they are not dead to holiness. He would have them feel strong in themselves, and cultivate self-righteousness. This is his strength of position, because it keeps the soul from Christ. As he hates holiness, he would remove the soul from Christ as far as possible; yet his main purpose is accomplished when he succeeds in preventing a holy union with him, which is a sure defeat of all his plans. Even if he be baffled in this, he does not relinquish his attempts upon those united to Christ, but rather entertains a peculiar hatred towards them on account of their very connection with him in holiness. His subtlety and art in deceiving render it much more important that we should watch our hearts, and discriminate concerning the working of our affections towards God and man. We are taught not to "believe every spirit, but to try the spirits whether they are of God." Many false views of Christ and of his work in the soul are afloat, which render discrimination and vigilance absolutely necessary, if we would guard against being deceived. The apostle says, "Be sober, be vigilant; because your adversary the devil, as a roaring lion, walketh about, seeking whom he may devour; whom resist, steadfast in the faith." (1 Pet. 5:8.) "Put on the whole armor of God, that ye may be able to stand against the wiles of the devil." (Eph. 6:11, 12.) He was ready to encounter the Saviour in person, and his efforts were especially prominent, when the Saviour was upon earth, in his taking peculiar possession of men; yet we know the triumph of Christ over him, when tempted in person, and that by his word "the devil came out of those who were possessed of him." Christ, then, has complete power over him, being able to subdue his reign in the soul; and for this purpose was he manifested, to overcome and destroy his works. It is said, "Resist the devil and he will flee from you;" but we must resist him "steadfast in the faith," if we would be successful. We shall surely be baffled by him if we go forth to the encounter in our own unaided strength. Of this we are constantly reminded, and directed to put on the whole armor of God. In Christ is this perfect armor, with which we may engage in the battle and be certain of victory; but we must be girded with the entire armor, so as to be completely sheltered in him.

Whatever view we may take of the conflict between sin and holiness, we can but learn the weakness of the flesh, and the strength which we acquire in Christ to meet it. This was so deeply felt by the apostle, and the consciousness of it so controlled his whole life, that, as the result of his experience, he says, " I am crucified with Christ; nevertheless I live: yet not I, but Christ liveth in me; and the life which I now live in the flesh, I live by the faith of the Son of God, who loved me and gave himself for me." (Gal. 2: 20.) While we are in the flesh, we are entirely dependent upon Christ for life with God. "Without me," says the Saviour, " ye can do nothing. As the branch cannot bear fruit of itself, except it abide in the vine, no more can ye, except ye abide in me." (John 15:4.) The corruptions of our nature are so deep-seated, that they can be overcome and subdued only by that almighty power which comes from Him who first gave new life to the soul. " He is the good shepherd; he gave his life for the sheep," and he will defend them from all their enemies. Having given his life to redeem them, he will most assuredly take care of them; but for this, they must abide in him in faith. He says, " My sheep hear my voice, and I know them, and they follow me; and I give unto them eternal life; and they shall never perish, neither shall any man pluck them out of my hand." (John 10 : 27, 28.) Nothing can be more comforting than the perfect security of those who confide their souls to Jesus. By virtue of their union with him he becomes " the Shepherd and Bishop of their souls." He says, " I know my sheep, and am known of mine." Nothing can equal the tender love of Christ for those united to him in holiness; and shall we not continue to trust in that love? We know his voice of infinite compassion, speaking peace to the soul when burdened with a sense of sin; we found him ready to take our guilt away, and to impart new life; and shall we not continue to confide in him to sustain that life so freely given, and to defend it against the assaults of all its foes? " Having begun in the spirit," let us not feel that this spiritual life can be " made perfect by the flesh." We know these are contrary, the one to the other. The new spiritual life received from Christ is opposed to " the old man, which is still corrupt ; " and, as the deceitful workings of the latter can be reached only by the piercing power of the Holy Sanctifier, faith in Christ is ever necessary for the maintenance of the new life.

Of Bible-saints faith in Christ is as prominent a characteristic as their self-distrust. The two are ever found in unison. They clung to Christ because they felt their own deficiency. They did not imagine that they had "already attained, either were already perfect;" but, on the contrary, he who has unfolded the fullest experience of the new life, and who had participated in its highest joys, when enjoying the sublimest degree of holy exercise, even when "caught up to the third heaven, into paradise," and when he "heard unspeakable words,"—in the midst of this beatitude—nay, on account of it—needed "at horn in the flesh, the messenger of Satan to buffet him, lest he should be exalted above measure." This "thorn in the flesh" was painful to bear; yet the Searcher of hearts, who alone knows what is best for his redeemed ones, saw that it was needful in his case, as indeed it ever is for those who are elevated to the most exalted Christian experience, that they may be kept in their true position before the throne of grace. Yet, says the loving Saviour, "My grace is sufficient for thee," to enable thee to overcome those temptations and infirmities of the flesh, and thereby to secure growth in the divine life; and the beloved one could assert, "My strength is made perfect in weakness." From discipline and holy instruction such as this, the apostle had so thoroughly learned his own weakness for holiness, and the connection which this feeling of weakness had with strength from Christ, that he would not glory in any thing pertaining to himself, " except in his infirmities." He would, indeed, " most gladly glory in his infirmities, that the power of Christ might rest upon him." There was such a disposition to exalt self, that he even took pleasure in those things, however painful, which serve to counteract this disposition. When he felt weak in himself, he was strong in the power of Christ. (2 Cor. 12: 9.)

VI.

UNION WITH CHRIST IN HOLINESS THE FOUNDATION FOR GOOD WORKS.

THUS far we have examined the work of Christ, as developed in the believer's inner life. We have seen that the great object of the Redeemer's mission was to effect a reconciliation between God and man; that inasmuch as men, as a race, are in a state of moral alienation from God, being utterly destitute of holiness, Christ came as a remedy; and that in the accomplishment of his work in the believing soul the Holy Spirit produces a great spiritual change, of so holy a nature — partaking, as it does, of his moral likeness — that it lays the foundation for holy exercises towards God and man.

We are now prepared to take another view of the nature of this glorious work. In our investigation hitherto we have been impelled to the conclusion, that the believer is thus transformed in his moving springs of action, that there may be a foundation for good works; and that he is fitted for righteous works *only* by virtue of his union with Christ; since the change inwrought

THE FOUNDATION FOR GOOD WORKS. 101

is after the image of Christ. It is Christ-like as it is developed towards God and man. As Christ, from the infinite fulness of his love, acted out good will towards man, so do his children resemble him in such action: by reason of their union with him they partake of the same spirit. Christ says, "That which is born of the Spirit is Spirit." In its essence it is like Him that begat; and being implanted in the soul in the new life, it will go out in benevolent action. Christ "came, not to condemn the world, but to save." But in salvation the soul is unreservedly committed to him to follow implicitly his teachings. As Redeemer he has set up a kingdom which is thoroughly reformatory, not only in its nature as inwrought, but emphatically in the character of its principles. The prophet asks, "Who may abide the day of his coming? And who shall stand when he appeareth? For he is like a refiner's fire and like fullers' soap. And he shall sit as a refiner and purifier of silver, and shall purify the sons of Levi, and purge them as gold and silver, that they may offer unto the Lord an offering in righteousness." (Mal. 3: 2, 3.)

The great design of this purifying process is to prepare us "to offer unto the Lord an offering in righteousness." There are very many who would value good works, yet see no necessity for this purifying process. They cannot understand why God should not be pleased with their offering without it. Being, as they think, well disposed towards their fellow-men, when led to perform kind offices towards them, they cannot comprehend why God should not accept such acts as righteous. They fail to realize that God is an infinitely holy Being, and that as such he cannot be pleased with an unholy offering, and that his estimation of righteousness is very different from that of sinful man. Here is the radical difference between those who rest upon Christ's righteousness for good works and those who, in one form or another, are trusting to their own righteousness. This self-trust evidently assumes widely differing aspects. Some rely upon Christ to *help* them in their culture; others rely upon their own efforts exclusively; still they agree in rejecting God's purifying process for producing good works, the whole design of which is " to purify unto himself a peculiar people, zealous of good works." (Tit. 2 : 14.)

This great doctrine of spiritual purification was revealed at the time the first announcement of the Saviour was made. Very much in the religious observances of the Jews taught the necessity of this spiritual cleansing. And yet but few understood its practical design. Such, in the observance of those sacred rights, looked to the Atoning Sacrifice for purification and cleansing, as well as for forgiveness. God's covenant people, to whom these abundant promises and revelations concerning the Messiah's kingdom were made, evidently comprehended very little of the nature of that kingdom; and we find that, after his coming, his immediate disciples, aided as they were by all his instructions as to its nature, remained enveloped in much darkness relative to the subject until he had finished his work, ascended to the mediatorial throne, and sent the Comforter to guide them into all truth. Then, indeed, they saw that "his kingdom was not of this world," and that, being holy in its nature, it was not in accordance with the natural principles in man. They had the true spirit of his kingdom in their hearts, but their minds were so thoroughly imbued with the opinion then current among the Jews, that the Messiah was to be a temporal prince, that these prejudices were not removed until they were more deeply illuminated by the Spirit.

Even now, with all the accumulated light which we have upon the subject, much ignorance appears to prevail regarding it. We are not liable to fall into the old Jewish error respecting a temporal kingdom. It is generally admitted that it is spiritual; but as to the nature of that spirituality much error seems to exist.

The fact that he set up a kingdom in which the true spiritual reign of God is recommenced and established in the hearts of the redeemed, is, even as yet, but dimly comprehended. That his laws are to be obeyed, is very generally granted; but that his work of redemption, when accomplished in the believer's heart, lays the only foundation for true obedience to God, receives but comparatively little practical attention. There are but few who are ready practically to admit that "they that are in the flesh cannot please God," in the true import of that assertion as made by the Saviour when he says, "That which is born of the flesh is flesh" — is of such a nature that a new spiritual birth is needed to lay the foundation for obedience to the laws of his kingdom.

His kingdom "comes not with observation." The native pride of the heart, with its self-righteous complacency, always tends to overlook and undervalue its true nature. Coming, as it does, without observation by the outward view of natural men, it can never be correctly imitated by any invention of man, although many attempts at such imitation have been made. It consists not in the sad and demure countenance, in the external self-denial of the flesh, in any outward form of religious observance, or in the training and cultivation of the natural man. "The kingdom of God is within you," says the Saviour; and we have seen in what sense it is within, and who is to be received in the soul as King. In receiving Christ as our Saviour, we receive him as our King. By virtue of our union with him we become his willing subjects, and as his kingdom is set up in the heart by abasing self, so it is carried on upon the same principle.

Christ has promulgated laws for the government of his subjects, which are to be obeyed and carried out in all the acts, duties, and relations of life. It is true, that in his work of redemption he came to fit souls for heaven as the great and ultimate end, and that such work will not be completed in the subjects of it until the soul leaves these vile bodies and ascends to the blessed mansions; but souls are to be fitted for the society of heaven by becoming willing and obedient subjects of the reign of the Redeemer here. Says the Saviour, "Ye are my friends if ye do whatsoever I command you;" and, "Herein is my Father glorified, that ye bear much fruit; so shall ye be my disciples." (John 15: 14.) "He that heareth these sayings of mine, and *doeth* them, is likened unto a wise man."

These sayings were embraced in his Sermon on the Mount, which is a summary of the laws governing the subjects of his kingdom. The strictness of Christian practice which he therein urges upon his followers, is in exact accordance with the moral law, and is not to be received in the form of self-inflicted penance, but as embodying the essentials of spiritual and holy discipline which every one must undergo who is transformed by the Holy Ghost from one of the children of this world to one of the children of light. The utter renunciation of self — the surrender of all vanity — the patient endurance of all wrongs — the crucifixion of all natural and worldly desires — the absorption of all our interests and passions in the enjoyment of God — and the subordination of all that we do and all that we feel and say to his glory and the good of man; these form the leading virtues therein required, that we may be enabled to control all our active relations towards God and man. What a blessed world will this be, when these laws of Christ are carried out in all the details of life! And the time is coming in the history of our world when these holy principles will become the governing principles throughout its entire extent; for our Redeemer has commenced no uncertain work in the establishment of his kingdom. But how can this glorious result be attained while those who are professedly laboring for it persist in disregarding so greatly Christ's method of reform?

By all nominal Christians much stress is

placed upon good works towards man. The question, therefore, necessarily arises, What are good works with God? and what his method of securing them? For, notwithstanding there are such high encomiums on good works, we find a great difference in opinion as to what constitutes good works in God's estimation. Works which men laud as very good, entitling them even to heaven, are condemned by God as worthless. The Saviour forewarned us, when announcing his laws, that he will discriminate among works that are done for him in his name; indeed, in the reiteration of those laws, he discriminates, in a searching manner, between self-righteous works and the righteousness which is of God; asserting, at the conclusion, that many at the last day will claim to have done "many wonderful works," to whom he will say, "I never knew you." Their works would not have his image enstamped upon them, and therefore would not be acknowledged; while others would be rewarded with, "Come, ye blessed, inherit the kingdom prepared for you from the foundation of the world;" and this because their works had been performed unto him relative to the persons of his redeemed ones. If, then, such value is placed upon good works by the Saviour in his gospel system, it is all-important to understand what will be owned by him as such.

We witness the most striking exhibition of the estimation which he places upon good works in the sufferings which he endured to enable us to perform them; for in our examination we have found that union with Christ in the new creation, which lays the only foundation for good works, comes to us through his sufferings and death. As we hear from our suffering Saviour the agonizing cry, "Father, if it be possible, let this cup pass from me," accompanied with the submissive, "If it may not pass from me, except I drink it, thy will be done,"—how precious to know that we, too, can partake of the obedient spirit thus manifested by our glorious Substitute, and that the foundation for such participation is laid in the new spiritual life imparted by him! The spirit of the new life is the spirit of obedience to God; and true, filial, holy obedience comes only from that source.

This truth is forcibly exemplified in the conversion of the apostle Paul. When the Saviour appeared to him as he was on his way to Damascus to make known his will, it was by the Lord's revealing himself *in him* that he became " obedient to the heavenly vision." Till that moment he had not possessed the spirit of true obedience; but now the first breathing of his desire is, "Lord, what wilt thou have me to do?" Not that he had not before chosen the service of

God; for none were more strict than he in religious observance. Not that he was not zealous and laborious in his works towards God, but that his zeal and labors were not of the right quality. From his own words we learn that the grand defect with him previously had been, that whatever he did for God in his attempted obedience was done to establish his own righteousness. He was ignorant of the righteousness which God required, because satisfied with his own. He felt that he could obey God; that he had sufficient life in himself to enable him to live unto God, and did not feel that he was dependent upon an Infinite Saviour to give him that life which would enable him to live in obedience to him. (See Rom. ch. 7.) Feeling this confidence in himself, he had not submitted himself unto the righteousness of God. (Rom. 10 : 3.) Herein was the glaring deficiency in the discharge of his religious duties towards God, as he himself abundantly assures us in his Epistles; and it was not until he saw that he was so entirely destitute of holiness that there was no foundation for good works, that he yielded himself to Christ, and became a partaker of his righteousness. Upon this theme he loved to dwell; and he has declared very distinctly how it is, that "we are made the righteousness of God" *in Christ*.

He says, "For by grace are ye saved through faith; and that not of yourselves. It is the gift of God. Not of works, lest any man should boast. For we are his workmanship, created in Christ Jesus unto good works, which God hath before ordained that we should walk in them." (Eph. 2 : 8-10.) No language could more distinctly assert that the foundation for good works is laid in the soul by our being created in Christ Jesus, and thus united to him in holiness, and becoming loyal subjects of his kingdom and obedient to its laws.

That we may perceive how it is that the subjects of Christ's kingdom alone have the spirit of obedience, let us revert again to the nature of the obedience required. The Saviour has given us an epitome of it: "Thou shalt love the Lord thy God with all thy heart, and with all thy soul, and with all thy strength, and with all thy mind; and thy neighbor as thyself. This do, and thou shalt live." (Luke 10 : 27, 28.) Yes — if a man in his natural state can live according to this law, we have Christ's assurance that he shall have life with God. The love therein enjoined we ought to render. God is worthy of it, and his law is worthy of our entire and hearty obedience. We must all pronounce it good; and we can here learn what will make us acceptable to God. Do any feel in their hearts that they come up to this standard? Can any mortal think so? However this may be, the apostle settles the question decisively. He says, "Now, we know that whatsoever things the law saith, it saith to them who are under the law; that every mouth may be stopped, and all the world become guilty before God. Therefore by the deeds of the law there shall no flesh be justified in his sight; for by the law is the knowledge of sin." (Rom. 3 : 19, 20.)

Such testimony from God — and it is scattered in profusion throughout his word — ought to settle the question with us, that in his estimation we cannot be justified by an observance of the law. If any feel competent to meet its demands, they only array themselves against the testimony of God. Are they prepared to meet the righteous Judge on such an issue?

This law is God's immutable standard of good works, and all who are out of Christ must stand or fall in accordance with it; must be judged by it at the last day, and meet its awful penalties. We cannot conceive how any one can rightly understand the description of the blessings of those who partake of Christ's righteousness, without being struck with the contrast afforded by the unrighteous in the same connection. Does the Saviour hold up to view the glorious salvation of the believer? He at the same time contrasts it with the damnation of the unbeliever. When we are invited to look at the joys of "eternal life," we are also pointed to the miseries of "eternal death." While delineating the heavenly privileges of the "children of light," the attention is directed to those "in outer darkness." As the one class will be greeted with, "Come, ye blessed of my Father, inherit the kingdom prepared for you," the other must hear, "Depart, ye cursed, into everlasting fire, prepared for the devil and his angels!" And this fearful contrast is presented as the inevitable result of the spiritual condition of the two classes in their relations to God. As the believer, by virtue of his union with Christ, "hath everlasting life," so the unbeliever, from the nature of his spiritual condition, "cannot see life, but the wrath of God abideth on him." Here we see the great practical value of the work of redemption in its application to the believer. "Christ has redeemed from the curse of the law, being made a curse for us;" and in doing it, "its righteousness is fulfilled."

The apostle says, "Wherefore, my brethren, ye also are become dead to the law by the body of Christ, that ye should be married to another, even to him who is raised from the dead, that ye should bring forth fruit unto God." (Rom. 7:4.) Here the believer's union with Christ is set forth under the figure of the marriage relation.

Christ is the great deliverer from the demands of violated law. In him that law is so completely fulfilled and magnified, that its force for condemnation to the believer is destroyed. Sheltered in Him who is the accepted substitute, he is shielded from its penalties. But his acceptance is not the cold recognition which some would represent, but in the consummation of the sacred nuptial ties he is so united to the risen Saviour by the Spirit's work in him, that he partakes of his nature and personal righteousness, "that he may bring forth fruit unto God." This is its crowning excellence — that "the righteousness of the law is fulfilled" in the new spiritual life thus received. (Rom. 8:4.) "The carnal mind " — that is, the mind unrenewed by the Spirit — "is enmity against God; for it is not subject to the law of God, neither indeed can be." (Rom. 8:7.) It can never be subject to the law of God till it is born of the Spirit. "If ye know that he is righteous, ye know that every one that doeth righteousness is born of him." (1 John 2:29.) In the reception of the new life the germ is received, which in its nature contains the spirit and excellence of the law, from which, through the Spirit, arise those holy affections that are acceptable to God and lead to holy action.

Most precious fruit must come from a union

thus formed. Nothing can exceed the beauty and force of the language used in describing the affection which God entertains towards his redeemed people on account of this endearing relation. It is represented as greatly exceeding the affection of the tender mother for her beloved offspring; as being, indeed, so tenderly strong that he says, "Whoso toucheth thee toucheth *the apple of my eye.*" How interesting, then, to know that this peculiar attachment to them is on account of the righteousness of which they partake in this holy union with the Redeemer! The Scriptures abound in such expressions as, "I will betroth thee unto me forever; yea, I will betroth thee unto me in righteousness" — figuratively illustrating the love which our Heavenly Father entertains for the righteousness which his chosen ones share, from their peculiar relation to him in the new life. The very law which he will enforce against all those out of Christ, which contains as a penalty eternal exclusion from his presence, Christ, who has become the believer's righteousness, now enables them, through this new relation, to love and to follow, as the lasting characteristic of his redeemed family.

It is not enough, however, that, by reason of our possessing this holy principle of obedience, we have the heavenly disposition of a true child;

for, if we are truly his children, we shall put ourselves in holy training for the exercises and joys of this great spiritual household. It is a great thing to have the spirit of a truly obedient child of God; but, having that spirit, and in order to know that we do indeed bear that intimate relation, we must constantly cleave unto "the Lord our righteousness" by a living, active, holy obedience to his commands. When the Saviour was asked, "What shall we do that we might work the works of God?" his answer was, "This is the work of God, that ye believe on him whom he hath sent." (John 6 : 28, 29.) We have seen that works approved by God as righteous have their beginning in faith; and faith in God is a work, inasmuch as it unites the soul in holiness to him from whom flow those exercises and acts that God approves.

The teachings of the apostle are of the same purport. "For in Christ Jesus neither circumcision availeth any thing, nor uncircumcision, but a new creature." (Gal. 6 : 15.) "For in Christ Jesus neither circumcision availeth any thing, nor uncircumcision, but faith that worketh by love." (Gal. 5 : 6.) And again: "Circumcision is nothing, and uncircumcision is nothing; but keeping the commandments of God." (1 Cor. 7 : 19.) We learn hence, that a true interest in Christ does not consist in any outward observances or forms of worship, or in any external obedience, but in that faith which works by love in the new creature.

The result will first manifest itself in love to God; and this love will, from its very nature, go out in good will to man, thus leading us to keep the commandments of God. Indeed, so truly and instinctively do faith, love, and holy obedience blend together in the divine life in the soul, that, if our faith does not produce fruits of righteousness as the result, it is thereby shown not to be that faith which unites to Christ. Thus the Scriptures teach, and thus it must be from the nature of the work within. That faith, which is the special gift of God in the work of salvation, will produce good works, is forcibly maintained by the apostle James, when he urges upon the professed followers of Christ the necessity of good works as the fruit of this faith in Jesus. "Of his own will begat he us with the word of truth, that we should be a kind of first fruits of his creatures." (Jas. 1 : 18.) He speaks of the new birth in its connection with good works as does the apostle Paul — that they were begotten of God in the new life that they might bring forth fruits of righteousness; and that, to accomplish this, they must be "doers of the word, and not hearers only;" for, if they were hearers only, they were certainly deceiving themselves as to their having a true and saving interest in Christ. To be his in truth, is "to receive with meekness the ingrafted word;" which, being thus ingrafted, was able to save their souls. He further says, "Hearken, my beloved brethren: hath not God chosen the poor of this world, rich in faith, and heirs of the kingdom which he has promised to them that love him?" (Jas. 2:5.) He thus points them to their high elevation from the depths of poverty and sin to be heirs of the kingdom, holding up before them, by way of warning, certain ungodly practices, and showing them that these were entirely at variance with their exalted calling as followers of Jesus. They might talk of being saved by faith; but it was a dead faith, not having that life-giving power in it which accompanied the faith which is from God as his peculiar gift. With much force of reasoning he asks, "What doth it profit, my brethren, though a man say he hath faith, and hath not works? Can faith save him?" (Jas. 2:14.) Evidently the faith which unites the soul to Christ, in the saving efficacy of his righteousness, differs from such both in its nature and its practical results. There are, as we know, different kinds of faith, having reference to distinct objects. "The devils believe and tremble;" but their faith produces no good fruits, and it is painfully true that there is much faith in the world of no better nature.

The faith which unites to Jesus in holiness has direct reference to obedience, and that is the end which it accomplishes. The apostle cites Abraham's faith in offering up his son Isaac as being of the right kind, and treats of his obedience as so intimately connected with his faith, and so immediately resulting from it, as to blend them together as one act. He asks, "Was not Abraham justified by works, when he had offered Isaac his son upon the altar? Seest thou how faith wrought with his works, and by works was faith made perfect?" (Jas. 2:21, 22.) His faith and his obedient spirit were as closely connected as the foundation and the superstructure which rises on that foundation. When he yielded obedience to the requirement made of him, his whole soul rested in God's faithfulness. The command affected the darling object of his natural affections, and in his compliance with it he gave his whole heart to the reign of God. He so rested in God that he went cheerfully forward in his work of obedience; and when asked by his son the touching question, "Where is the lamb for a burnt-offering," his confiding spirit prompts the reply, "God will provide himself a lamb." Did not the father of the faithful understand the true import of the sacrificial lamb? Upon it his soul reposed in his relations to God, and through Jesus, the Lamb of God, he received the quickening, vitalizing power which flows from him. His example thus illustrates the nature of true faith and true obedience, showing that they are inseparably connected together.

Those religious teachers, who disparage Christian faith while pleading for Christian conduct, show about as much wisdom for the end to be accomplished as would a builder who should think to commence his building at the top, trusting to the winds of heaven to buoy it up. The great Teacher in Christian morals warns us against such instruction. He would produce beautiful fruits of righteousness by ingrafting the soul in himself through holy faith, and then would nourish and support this heavenly plant by the same life-giving faith from which it first derived its spiritual vitality. It will not grow and become fruitful unless it draws its nutriment from the parent stock. He says, "As the branch cannot bear fruit of itself, except it abide in the vine, no more can ye, except ye abide in me."

Fruitfulness is the end to be attained. This stands out prominent in every view which we take of Christ's reformatory work. However important it may be to secure a firm and enduring foundation, its practical value consists in the structure which is reared upon it. We have seen the intimate connection between holy faith and works of righteousness and the heaven-born love in union with Christ, by which faith works; and we know of no hidden "life with God within" that is not directly connected with an outward manifestation in regulating the conduct towards man. We may be very sure that we have not true love in exercise towards God while we manifest ill will towards man; that we are not righteous and honest with him while unrighteous and dishonest with man. The great lesson to learn is, how to "add to faith virtue, and to virtue knowledge, and to knowledge temperance, and to temperance patience," and all the graces of the Spirit and all the outward adornings in "whatsoever things are honest, lovely, and of good report." Christ reforms the subjects of his kingdom so thoroughly that the spirit and temper of their hearts may meet the approval of God, and their "good fruit commend itself to men.". "By their fruits ye shall know them;" and he regenerates and sanctifies and holds them up before the world as "a city set upon a hill." They are "the light of the world," and they are to reflect the light they receive from him, "that others may see their good works, and glorify their Father which is in heaven."

In this feeling Christ's disciples heartily join. It stimulates them to action ; and in their labor, and for the disposition for righteous labor, they " glorify God." It is this that most of all distinguishes their works from all self-righteous doing. They glorify God that Christ has so *wrought in them*, that they may share with him in his holy benevolence while diffusing it to others. We find Bible Christians, in giving their experience, in " abundant labors," for Christ, are very particular to point to the source whence it emanated. It is " not I, but the grace of God, which was with me." When contrasting attainments made in " divine life " with former degradation, it is said, " By the grace of God, I am what I am." And when referring to the controlling purpose of life, we are pointed to Christ's *work within* as the source, saying, " The life I now live in the flesh I live by the faith of the Son of God." They were alive unto God, because the flesh was " crucified with Christ," so that it is " not I, but *Christ liveth in me*." Thus right doing with them is the " righteousness of God by faith ; " and as faith is thus a mighty working power, they would cut off all idea of human merit, by assuring those they addressed, that this kind of faith is " not of yourselves ; it is the gift of God."

This feeling is in marked contrast with those

who feel confident in their *own power* for works of righteousness, and who feel no true dependence for a life within, "hid with Christ in God," as the foundation of righteousness.

There is a vast difference, whether the union is formed by Christ's uniting our souls to him in his holiness, or by our uniting ourselves to him in an imitation of his righteousness in outward religious duties — a difference that lays the foundation for the joys of eternal life or the miseries of eternal death. Yet it is not for man to call to account for it. The laws of human society are not violated by the difference. Men may be amiable and lovely in the various relations of life, and ornaments of the society in which they move. In the discharge of their religious duties it is not for man to detect whether they have only " a name to live " when in reality they are dead, or whether they are truly " alive unto God." " Should I give all my goods to feed the poor," can man complain of the act, because it does not proceed from love to God? Plainly, it is not his province to judge his neighbor in respect to the righteousness of the act; and yet in our relations to God it is of vital importance, and the means of knowing are within our reach; since God has clearly taught that if it flow not from holy love, it will not be owned by him. (1 Cor. ch. 13.) It is not, therefore, before a human tribunal that we are to try our work, but at the tribunal of Him "who judgeth in righteousness" according to his own standard, where it will be of no avail to plead that our works were done for him, if he does not know us as those he has "washed from sins in his own blood."

Another distinguishing characteristic of those whom Christ reforms, and which makes them efficient for good works, is *their adherence to his laws*. This, as we have seen, is the spirit of his reform. The spirit and essence of the new life, received at the spiritual birth, are according to the spirit of the moral law. But as this Heaven-born principle is in conflict with corruptions of the heart which still remain, and is contested in its working at every step by "the world, the flesh, and the devil," in the manifold forms of "the lusts of the flesh, the lusts of the eye, and the pride of life," we see the wisdom and tender care of the Good Shepherd in giving such abundant instruction, adapted to all the relations of life. He would thus guard his flock and encircle them in his fold by giving them specific directions to meet every condition in which his providence may place them. This is a source of great comfort to his people. They hear his caution, "Believe not every spirit, but try the spirits whether they be of God." Their experience has taught them the necessity of such caution, and they rejoice in the numerous tests which he has given in his word. They acknowledge no inward monitor, whether by nature or grace, to be followed as a sure guide, unless it conforms to his written word. Theirs is not a spirit that follows natural impulses and visions of the imagination, but it adheres implicitly to the laws prescribed. He who is united to Christ so as to "walk with God in newness of life," will walk according to his *revealed* will. The spirit thus received is the reverse of a self-confident spirit. Being received through self-abasement, its subject is prepared to walk humbly and carefully, and at each advancing step he looks up to his Saviour to inquire, "Lord, what wilt thou have me to do?" desiring most of all that his acts may please him; and confiding in him for his spirit to enlighten, he takes his word as the unerring standard for all right doing.

The subjects of Christ's kingdom are law-abiding citizens. Those loyal to him are from their very nature loyal to civil government. They greatly value it as regulating the conduct of man towards his fellow; they acknowledge it as ordained by the word of God as indispensable to the well-being of society; they prize the good order which results from it when it is rightly administered, and feel the obligations of doing what they can to make it conform to God's principles of justice and equity. In their civil and social relations they adhere to law; and yet Christ's laws with them are supreme. When there is an unmistakable conflict between the civil law and the plain law of Christ, and the question arises, which is to be obeyed, there can be no parleying on their part as to the path of duty; they will take the consequences of a firm adherence to the laws of God. This must be so, from the relation they sustain to him. Although from it they cherish a superior respect for "the powers that be," as ordained of God, yet what are earthly powers — kings or presidents — if in their enactments they conflict with the Infinite and Supreme? The laws of their spiritual King are of supreme obligation with them, not only from a conviction of the transcendent importance of such laws to society, but from an inward and deep-seated love of their benevolent nature and designs. We are aware that this principle may be perverted, and when so wrested be instrumental in producing much mischief in society. But what benevolent principle may not? Men may plead for Christ's higher law, when in reality it is their own higher law; and if self-will takes the helm, it steers not in the channel of God's righteousness, though it be baptized in his name.

In the new creation the laws of God are said to be "put into the heart." "This is the covenant that I will make with them after those days, saith the Lord; I will put my laws into their hearts, and in their minds will I write them." (Heb. 10:16.)

A love of the commands of Christ becomes, then, a prominent feature in the character of those who partake with him of his righteousness. From their union with him they imbibe a true love of his reign. In his instructions to them concerning prayer, the first petition is, "Thy kingdom come — thy will be done — as in heaven, so on earth." This is first in importance, and has the first place in their hearts.

As their best and strongest affections centre in their Redeemer, so his commands, being, like himself, the embodiment of good will to man, become the controlling objects of their strong desires; and this spirit is greatly strengthened and improved by acting it out in conformity to revealed laws. Does any one object that such a principle actively at work in society would be dangerous to the best interests of civil government? On the contrary, would it not be — is it not — the best friend of those interests? Was not our Redeemer a friend of civil government? And do not those who partake of his spirit for the extension of his laws, follow him in this respect, as well as in all others? They may, indeed, be compelled to disregard a particular edict of civil government, from a supreme regard to his laws; but they are not on that account to be regarded as the foes of such government. It may well be that their very disregard of this particular edict will do more than all else to make the government worthy of respect. They may be called to suffer the penalty of their disobedience, and be subjected to reproach as evil doers; but that does not make them such. Happily, in our land this principle has so far moulded civil government in conformity with natural justice and equity, that we know comparatively little of suffering for righteousness' sake, except in connection with a system of barbarism in a portion of it, which has been permitted to grow up in our midst and pervert the benevolent designs of our civil and religious institutions. Of course, such a system, founded in injustice, and yet strengthened and perpetuated by civil law, must come in collision with the laws of God.

It is not strange, therefore, that those who are laboring to make such a system perpetual, should scoff at "the higher law"—a principle to whose influence we are indebted for one of the best forms of civil government on the face of the earth. Certainly its friends need not despond, when they look back and see what its benign power has accomplished in the improvement of civil government since Christ formally set up his kingdom. Although selfishness may prompt some to rail and scoff at it, yet let Christ's followers, with an eye of faith, lay hold of the sure word of prophecy, which affords us such abundant assurance that his principles must triumph and prevail over all forms of selfishness. When they shall so pervade society as to become diffused throughout all the workings of civil government, whose every enactment shall then be founded in justice and righteousness, their exceeding great value will not fail to be seen and appreciated in elevating and blessing mankind in all their social and civil relations.

While it is important that we understand how to apply Christ's law to our civil relations, its relative importance must not be overlooked. In carefully examining the example and teaching of our Saviour in his life on earth, do we not find that he placed first in importance in our social relations. the more retiring and private duties? It is here that holy love has its most precious developments; in the family first of all, thence extending itself to our neighbor in the retired intercourse of life, and "in visiting the fatherless and widows in their affliction, and keeping ourselves unspotted from the world."

But in all our relations — whether the domestic or the more public — union with Christ in divine life can alone fit us to obey his general precept, "As ye would that men should do unto you, do ye even so unto them; for this is the law and the prophets."

Thus, in every view of Christ's work, we find that "a sceptre of righteousness is the sceptre of his kingdom." Is it not, then, an infinite privilege to surrender all our faculties to the control of such a Sovereign? Blessed sovereignty! which is exercised upon such conditions as to unite the loyal subjects of his kingdom in devoted labors for the extension of his dominion, and in a participation with him in his holy triumphs as he achieves his victories in the world!

VII.

CHRIST'S REFORM BEARING UPON THE INSTITUTION OF SLAVERY.

There is one form of sin, deeply seated in the human heart, to which Christ's reformatory principles are to be applied, that, from its peculiar manifestations in our country's history hitherto, and the astounding claims which have of late been put forth in its behalf, demands our special attention in this connection. We refer to the sin of oppression.

This manifests itself in a great variety of ways in its bearing upon the mental and physical condition of our race; but in whatever form it has its outgoing, it is hateful to God, and its spirit is in direct antagonism with the spirit of the gospel. Christ came to raise up the fallen, to give strength to the weak and helpless, and to deliver the oppressed. It is generally admitted that gospel principles are to be applied to the extirpation of this sin, as it is developed in the social and commercial relations of individuals; yet many seem to think that they are not to be brought to bear against organized, combined, and consolidated oppression. Can any one sincerely maintain the proposition, that Christ's principles of reform are to be made applicable to a sin, as exhibited in the individual while it is in comparatively a weak and feeble state, and yet are to be ignored when the same is embodied in an institution, and has become a gigantic enormity, legalized and protected by the sturdy arm of the civil law?

It has been often asserted by Christians that Christ and his apostles did not condemn slavery; and an argument for the strengthening and perpetuation of this institution is sought to be built upon this assumed fact. But is this, indeed, true? Let us look at the system, and see whether this opinion is rightly formed; for every Christian in these times should be able to give a reason founded upon Christian principles for his opinion upon a subject of such vital importance to the cause of Christ as well as to the best interests of our country. Should it be found, as we think it will, that the system of American slavery is a system of oppression, against which the ethics and spirit of the gospel are arrayed in unmistakable distinctness, Christ's followers would not need a more direct and specific condemnation of it by name in order to enlist their efforts and influences in the same direction.

It cannot be controverted that Christian principles had a powerful influence in shaping our present free government; nor can that government be preserved but by the same high regard for God and his government which actuated its early founders. When our fathers, through much toil and suffering, had succeeded in establishing upon this continent those principles of civil and religious liberty which, finding their manifestation in our present frame of government, are so admirably adapted to favor the growth of Christ's kingdom, the great enemy could not suffer those principles to have free and untrammelled scope, that they might thus reach their proper development; but, through avarice and other evil passions in man, succeeded in introducing, side by side with the same, a species of despotism in its most insidious and corrupting form; trusting to so intermingle it in our social, commercial, civil, and church relations, as through its means to mar the working of our beautiful system of government, and, if possible, to overthrow it ultimately. Now, fellow-Christians, look abroad in all portions of our country, and mark the result! Contrast the state of our country on this subject when our government was founded, and what a decided change does its present condition afford! Then the people of all sections were harmonious and *united under the government of their choice;* now, in a large portion of it, anarchy and rebellion reign. The most solemn covenants are trampled under foot, and high treason is applauded as a Christian virtue. The most sacred official trusts have been violated by high officials, who secretly and stealthily used the whole strength of their official power to introduce and extend this rebellion, — to accomplish which, public property has been most unscrupulously plundered, and such violation and such plunder are approved in a large section, and rewarded with the highest honors.

Now, what is the cause of this organized rebellion, with its accompaniments of perjury, robbery, theft, and wholesale corruption? What but slavery? However the different sections may disagree as to the right or the wrong of the institution, and however wide the disagreement in all sections as to the manner of dealing with it, yet all will now agree that this is the real cause of our present troubles.

Have those now in rebellion been driven to that rebellion by the oppressive acts of the government against which they are in revolt? Have those constitutional guarantees, under which the Union and the government were formed, been violated? No one can say, in truth, that any such excuses can be interposed in behalf of the rebels. Have their local and state laws, which recognize property in slaves, and afford protection to it, been in the slightest degree infringed? Not in the least. What, then, is the real gist of the trouble? Simply this — that the rebels feared that, under the government as it might be administered hereafter, they might be restricted in their desire to extend slavery beyond its constitutional limits. This is the extent of the oppression of which complaint was made. It is that their purpose of extending this system of oppression over others cannot have full scope, coupled — as, perhaps, the most galling consideration — with the consciousness that the conscientious convictions of a large majority of the people of the country are in decided hostility to this system.

Does it not become an important Christian duty, then, to investigate the nature of this system, and to compare it with the nature and principles of Christianity? This rebellion strikes a deeper blow at Christianity itself than at the government, even, against which it is arrayed. We are charged with an entirely false view of Christianity, when we talk of conscientious convictions against the righteousness of slavery; and this, not by a few leading rebellious spirits, but by the popular voice of the Christian ministry and the church within the limits of this rebellion. It becomes us, therefore, to ascertain whether we have a true view of Christianity in its application to this system.

Although at present the war has taken the subject very much out of the reach of moral influences, yet it becomes us, while feeling the scourge that is upon us, to review its *moral bearings*, that we may be prepared to meet it hereafter as becomes Christian citizens. As the government is conducting the war for the suppression of rebellion, and to enforce its laws, and not for emancipation, if it is successful, as we have reason to believe it will be, then it may become practically of the first importance to American Christians, that they be prepared to apply the *moral remedy* in the true spirit of *Christ's reform*. We turn our attention to the subject, with the feeling that, while we are right in our views of Christianity in its opposition to slavery, yet our opposition has been too much shaped and controlled by the spirit of the world; and that, in consequence of our *inaction* and *wrong* action, our nation is suffering the just judgment of God. Although slavery is a sectional institution, yet the sin by which we have connived at it, and nurtured it into its present magnitude for mischief, has been national. It is pleasing to notice the unanimity with which Christians in the loyal part of our country urge on a vigorous prosecution of the war, till the rebels are brought to an unconditional surrender; yet, when that is accomplished, they must be prepared to pour upon the belligerent elements the benign influence of the gospel; that, in their repentance for past sins, they may "bring forth fruits meet for repentance."

Without going into an extended examination of the iniquity of slavery in its practical working, it is sufficient to notice that the essence of its wrong consists in making man property. This is accomplished by human laws, according to which "slaves are deemed to be chattels personal, to all intents, purposes, and constructions whatsoever;" and "a slave is one doomed in his own person and his posterity to live without knowledge and without capacity to make any thing his own, and to toil that another may reap the fruits." Ponder well, then, the import of these fearful words—"slavery" and "slave"—in their practical results, and say if such a system can have any affinity with the benevolent laws of Christ's kingdom. The definitions above cited were not given by some fanatical abolitionist; they are taken from express decisions of judicial tribunals in the slaveholding states as to the legal construction of slavery. Is there an intelligent layman in the country who does not know that these definitions simply express the *practical workings* of the system in every particular?

If such be the legal construction of the system as promulged by its especial friends, who, assuredly, would have every inducement to present it in as favorable a light as possible, what is it but a system of oppression, as a whole and in every detail? By what other name than that of oppression can it be defined? How is it possible that any friend of Christ can so degrade the gospel system as to contend that it has any affinity with such a wrong? Who comes forward to advocate Christ's system as one which "dooms its subjects to live without knowledge," &c.? If such a man there be, he must be farther removed from gospel light than has ever come to our knowledge. There is, indeed, a style in vogue of advocating the principles of the gospel, and at the same time attempting to make them harmonize with slavery, which, though it is as far removed from the truth in its *results*, does not yet so directly war with all regard for common sense; for there is not a child in our Sabbath schools that does not know that every feature of the gospel system is calculated to elevate and bless, and that to impart light and knowledge is its grand design. Christ is "the light of the world," and those redeemed and regenerated by him are sent out *to impart light to others;* and "whosoever doeth truth cometh to the light, that his deeds may be made manifest that they are wrought in God." *Evil* doers are they "that love darkness rather than light."

While Christ's kingdom is advanced by diffusing light upon the mind in all possible ways, the slave system is directly antagonistic to it in this respect. Indeed, it would be extremely difficult to find any system that has its satanic origin more distinctly stamped upon it than has this. It cannot be sustained and extended but by darkening the mind. This cannot be denied, as it stands out prominently in every thing connected with it. It not only shuts out light and knowledge from the slave to such an extent that, in some states, at least, it is made by law a crime to teach a slave to read, but the same feature shows itself in every thing pertaining to it. It can live only by adhering tenaciously to this policy. We know that boasts are made of the liberality evinced in dealing out oral instruction to the slave, and would rejoice that through this channel they may often obtain a ray of light sufficient to point them to the only way of salvation; yet it is a repulsive thought, that in the midst of the meridian light which we enjoy, knowledge can come to any through such a channel *only*. Popery, too, has its oral instruction, by which it doles out its view of the gospel; but it has always been regarded by Protestants as a dark sign connected with the system, that it can only thrive through the ignorance of the mind. There is no organized system of iniquity upon the face of the earth that has been so afraid of the light as the system of slavery in our land. It has taken the lead of all others in its espionage over every avenue through which light can come, and with the utmost rigor shuts out every ray that will be likely to shine upon it. For the introduction of this rebellion, and to maintain its hold upon the community, outrages and crimes that would disgrace the most barbarous nations on earth have been committed against honest and peaceable citizens, for no other reason than their being suspected of harboring in their breast the true light of the gospel upon this system. Innocent and unoffending females have been most barbarously treated for no other reason. Cold-blooded murders have been frequent for this cause alone. Such deeds of darkness have not sprung up at once, and as the fruit of war; but for a long series of years they have been encouraged as the safeguards which the institution required. Although it would not be just to represent that the Christian community, in the midst of it, sanctioned such barbarous practices, yet, have they not sanctioned the policy of shutting out the light that should shine out against such wickedness?

But there is a source of more poignant grief than has yet been mentioned. This process of darkening the mind upon the subject of slavery has been going on so long and to such an extent, that the proclamation is now boldly made to the world that slavery is a divine institution, established by God himself, as " an organized element in that family order which lies at the very foundation of church and state." Its advocates speak of it as "an institution of which the church are God's appointed guardians;" they declare that the church has a trust " to conserve and perpetuate the institution of domestic slavery as now existing;" that " the nature and solemnity of the present trust are, to transmit our existing system of domestic servitude, with the right unchallenged by man to go and root itself wherever Providence and nature may carry it" — a trust so sacred and important to the well-being of man, that they " will discharge it, and not surrender it till the last man has fallen in its defence behind its last rampart." Those who would, in a peaceful and lawful way, prevent the spread of the system, are spoken of as "seeking to wrest from them [the slaveholders] their Heaven-given rights in their Heaven-allowed property."

Such views are not put forth in isolated cases; but a volume could be filled with precisely such sentiments recently published in different localities, and representing the general sentiment of the church in the section where the present rebellion reigns. The foregoing extracts are taken from the discourses of two eminent divines of the Presbyterian church, Dr. Palmer, of New Orleans, and Dr. Wilson, of Augusta, Ga.; and we could name eminent divines in the free states who appear to sympathize with such sentiments. They are appeals addressed to Christian men, urging it as an important Christian duty to guard and protect their " Heaven-given rights in their Heaven-allowed property." The general prevalence of such sentiments is but the legitimate fruit of the policy pursued by the church towards the institution. Every one, possessed of any intelligence whatever in relation to the subject, must know that such sentiments would have been repelled with abhorrence by the church in the slave states at the time our government was framed.

The poor slave, therefore, is not the only sufferer, if he is the greatest, from the unrighteous attempts made to darken the mind in order to sustain the institution. The master must come in for a large share of the injury inflicted; and who can recount the long train of injuries that follow?

Our investigation, however, leads us more particularly to notice the deep wound inflicted upon our holy religion. In this aspect a heart-rending spectacle is presented to the Christian. Ministers of Jesus, professed advocates of his Heaven-born benevolence, engaged in earnestly pleading for their "Heaven-given rights" to enslave their fellow-man! This, to a plain mind, uninitiated in the debasing process which has been these many years going on, appears passing strange. We can understand how one "born of the Spirit," and truly partaking of the benevolent disposition that flows from such birth, may remain, *for the time being*, in the legal relation of master, and yet give to his servants "that which is just and equal," according to Christ's higher law, and discharge his Christian obligations as perfectly as those who do not sustain that relation; yet we cannot understand how *the system* which makes men "chattels"—by which they are "doomed in their own person and their posterity to live without knowledge and without capacity to make any thing their own, and to toil that another may reap the fruit"—can have any affinity with the benevolence which Christ inculcates and the Holy Spirit imparts. What is there in such a system to commend it to the special regard of the Christian? What, that should commit to the Christian a special trust "to conserve and perpetuate" it? What, that should induce Christian ministers to advocate and stimulate rebellion against one of the best governments on earth?

Look at its practical working. Go visit the

slave marts common in all large towns where slavery reigns, and witness the distressing scenes of separation of husband and wife, of parents and children — and these are the common and legitimate fruits of the system — how is it possible for Christ's ministers to plead in its behalf? Is not the family relation to be held sacred and inviolate according to Christ's law? Does he not expressly say of that union which is its foundation, "What God hath joined together let not man put asunder"? And yet, according to the legal construction and the practical workings of the slave system, it is sundered. Can a slave have a wife of his bosom whom he can call his own? Is not that relation entirely at the will of his master? The master, from a regard to his own interest, may encourage what shall serve as a substitute for that relation; but the same interest impels him to tear it asunder when it is formed. Can a slave call his children his own? No; according to this system there is nothing to which the heart of man cleaves on earth that he can call his own. But, blessed be God! there is one Infinite Friend in heaven, and a treasure there that is secured to him beyond the reach of those unrighteous laws that doom him on earth "to live without the capacity to call any thing *his own.*" And yet such a system as this is held up before the world as "a great, beneficial, civilizing institution," and "one of the colored man's foremost sources of blessings," the conservation and perpetuation of which appeal to Christianity in its highest form; and all who would oppose and circumscribe it are to be disposed of summarily as infidels and fanatics!

We confess that this "higher form" of Christianity is as yet hidden from us. We have been looking at first principles, and so far every view which we have taken of their requirements and tendencies points to directly the reverse. We take a glimpse of the Christian life in its new, Heaven-born disposition towards God and man, and we find every feature of it at work to elevate and improve the degraded. There is nothing which looks like dooming them to a lasting degradation; and we believe that this disposition would lead the Christian to give to others just what the Saviour requires in the golden rule, and what he so much values in his own case — justice and liberty. We can discover no place where this "Heaven-given right" to enslave comes into the gospel system. Certainly, all specific instruction given to those in the relation under consideration, would lead them to work against it, and to abolish it, so far as lies within their power. Such, we believe, was the effect of that instruction in the first workings of Christianity; and such is its effect now, as Christian principles are acted out in relation to it.

We believe that the Christian who has drunk at the fount of spiritual life, whose soul is imbued with the love of Christ's holy principles, would require some better reason for adopting the slave code than any which its advocates have yet advanced. All their appeals to the Bible, which we have seen, wear the appearance of an attempt to lay hold of *an excuse* for their acts, rather than an earnest effort to discharge a high Christian obligation to do righteously. They sometimes appeal to "the curse pronounced upon the servants of Ham," and to the regulation in the Hebrew civil code which required them to take their bondmen from the heathen, and not from among the Hebrews.

Granting that the Africans are the descendants of Ham, what possible obligation can rest upon Christians in our day to carry out that curse? To go back so near the flood for an instance of God's retributive justice towards a particular people, can hardly be reckoned among the higher Christian obligations. It is our high calling to extend the Heaven-given *blessings* of Christianity; and God will take care of his own retributive justice towards nations, races, and individuals. If we send our missionaries to Africa, it is to extend the *blessings* of Christianity, and not to enslave the inhabitants, in order to carry out God's curse upon the descendants of Ham.

In reference to Hebrew servitude as regulated in their civil code, we know that there were other things besides slavery tolerated and regulated in the civil laws of that people, which conflicted with the eternal moral code, and which certainly should not be practised by us. Christ said that such practices were tolerated in their civil code by Moses "*for the hardness of their hearts.*" The kind of conduct which we need is that which is in accordance with Christ's laws, and comes from "pure hearts," and not such as was tolerated in the civil laws of the Hebrews on account of their "hardness of heart." Is it not indeed strange that Christians, and even eminent divines, should exalt this temporary regulation of the Jews over God's immutable law? If, in behalf of slavery, this Jewish code, never intended as a permanent regulation, is to take precedence of God's unchangeable moral standard of righteousness, why are not all its requirements relative to slavery adopted and observed? Why reject its merciful arrangements, and cling only to those features which are attributable to the hardness of heart of this people? Why are those provisions disregarded which abolished Hebrew servitude in the seventh and fiftieth years? Why is there no "year of Jubilee," as was the case in the Jewish system? If such features were observed, would not this zeal to perpetuate and extend the institution be essentially checked?

Such is the nature of the appeals made to Scripture invariably by the aiders and abettors of American slavery. How does it happen that in their extended biblical researches they have never, in a single instance, deemed it advisable to appeal to Christ's standard of righteousness—his holy precepts? These form the basis of all the teachings of the apostles in their instructions relative to this subject, as well as to every other. Why are they, then, set aside and disregarded? Is it not for the simple reason that the system which the apologists for American slavery defend, would be manifestly repudiated by the practice and precept of the Saviour? Who would think of applying these holy precepts for the purpose of extending and perpetuating such an institution as the one under consideration? To make such an application, except for the purpose of accomplishing the overthrow of this iniquity, would be trifling with common sense. And yet this is the *only* standard by which our actions are to be tried.

Grant that the slave is in a better condition than the African in his native country: is that a sufficient reason for withholding from him the beneficent treatment which the Saviour enjoins? Surely Christian morality is not to be gauged by heathenism. Nor is it right to distrust Christ's principles by pleading that the slave is "better off" than he would be if those principles were applied to accomplish his freedom. Has the Christian any warrant for such a distrust as is evinced by substituting laws which doom man to a degradation beyond all possibility of removal under their legitimate workings, in the place of those righteous laws, whose whole tendency is to elevate and reform? Have not human elevation and reform invariably resulted in all cases where the standard of righteousness has been faithfully applied? Then why distrust their application to this degraded people? What havoc is made with the holy doctrines and righteous practices which the gospel enjoins, by substituting man's standard of righteousness for God's!

A person residing in some portions of our country would think, from the laws of his state, as well as from the laws of Christ, that he ought to treat a black man with the same justice and equity as he would a white man. From a perusal of either he could form no conception that he had a "Heaven-given right" to oppress one more than the other. Christ's laws of justice and equity have so pervaded the community — the feeling that "there is no respect of persons with God" has taken such deep root among them from their religious training—that the civil law is shaped in conformity therewith; and the Christian and the infidel are alike trained to condemn the legalized oppression of any man, or class of men, on account of a difference in complexion or mental endowments. Suppose that same person takes up his residence in another portion of our land where he finds a radical distinction made between men, based upon difference in color and mental endowments. He finds that the same act, prompted by the same benevolent heart, that he had thought righteous in the state first mentioned, is branded in the latter as a crime; and if he give free utterance to the benevolent feelings of his heart, he will be confined in a prison with felons, or hung up according to Lynch law.

Has God's law of righteousness, however, changed by his removal from one state to another? Not "one jot or tittle." That does not change to suit the public sentiment of any community; and those who love righteousness have great reason to rejoice in the immutability of this standard. A true sense of it brings them to the foot of the cross and keeps them there; and the divine benevolence which flows therefrom goes out just as freely towards the degraded African as towards the Anglo-Saxon, and is of the same heavenly nature in one locality as in another.

We find that the Scriptures clearly enjoin it as a Christian duty, to sustain and respect human governments; yet we find nothing therein to indicate that their enactments can annul our obligations to God's moral government. Their jurisdiction must, from the nature of the case, be subordinate, inasmuch as their laws cannot reach the disposition of the heart, as the laws of God do; nor can they supersede the authority of the latter over the outward conduct. The condition of things in our country presents a forcible exemplification of the value of this truth in its bearing upon civil government. Looking abroad throughout our land, where is to be found the most sacred regard for civil obligations and constitutional government? Is it not where there is the strongest regard for "Christ's higher law"? And does not this fact demonstrate the truth that a true and controlling regard for that "higher law" is the best security for our civil government? We find no open rebellion against our government in the free states. There are spirits, indeed, that sympathize with the present rebellion, and who have lent a helping hand to fan its flames; but they are, in the main, such as openly advocate man's "higher law" as of supreme authority, and they are but few in number. How is it, on the other hand, in those states where for years the pulpit and the press have universally cast contempt upon Christ's "higher law"? There, as the natural and inevitable fruit, we have many states arrayed in open rebellion against the government, for the sole reason that they cannot extend this system of oppression. They, too, have a "higher law" — a law which makes men "chattels personal," and dooms them to an ignominious degradation — a law that separates husband and wife, parents and children, at the will of man, and they have only a contemptuous sneer for any *higher law* than this.

Is there not, then, occasion for us to take lessons at the feet of Jesus, that we may learn how to apply his holy principles, his "higher law," to this system? No imitation of it will meet the necessities of the case. To an unprejudiced mind, even a superficial view of his principles will disclose a "higher law" than the slave code; yet we need to come into true sympathy with "the law of spiritual life in Christ," that we may be prepared to counteract the pernicious influence of this code in all its complicated associations. Infidel reformers can see the iniquity of the system of slavery, and its antagonism to natural religion. They can severely denounce and criminate Christ's professed followers for their delinquencies in relation to it. All systems of false religion can join in this, and lay to their souls the flattering unction which self-righteousness prompts from their thus arraying themselves against such an unrighteous system. All this, however, fails to apply the adequate remedy; and we believe that nothing will effectually meet the corrupt workings of the system, *as now developed*, in a peaceful and effectual manner, but that supernatural benevolence which comes from a holy union with the great Reformer. His system of reform, rightly understood, will lead men not only to see the wrong and condemn it, but also to apply the heavenly antidote contained in that precious system.

That this remedy may be rightly applied, Christians need the exercise of the highest virtues of their holy religion. Fortunately, there is not only general instruction to meet the case, but we have the application of these benevolent principles to the institution by the apostles themselves. Let us, then, draw more largely from this storehouse, and see how they met the evil. They lived in the midst of it themselves, and knew well its unholy working; and it is our duty to adapt the principles they laid down to our circumstances. The specific instructions which we have from them on the subject will greatly facilitate our labors in this direction.

The first thing which strikes us when we turn our attention to this source is, that they inculcate the same high and heavenly benevolence in their instructions regarding this sin as they do regarding all other sins, and that they apply them in the same manner *to the individual conscience.* They do not attack systems of government and their laws, for the obvious reason that Christ's "kingdom is not of this world," and his laws reach beyond these systems to the heart of the individual believer. They dealt with sin in a practical manner, by applying the remedy to the seat of the disease.

In addressing instructions to the different churches formed in the midst of slavery under the Roman government, they do not dwell upon the wickedness of the slave system, and exhort them to use their influence and power for its suppression under that government, for the very plain reasons that they had no responsibility for Nero's despotism and oppression, and could exert no political influence or power over it. We are not, however, to infer from this that Christians under our government, for the laws enacted by which *they share with others an equal and common responsibility*, are not to use that responsibility, according to their constitutional power, in a Christian manner, to counteract the evils of this system under our government.

Although the subject has thus a political bearing, it must not be forgotten that this is ever subordinate to the higher. Is it not manifest that the great duty of the church at the present time is to learn to deal with the system in its religious and moral aspects? Political warfare, as conducted in our day, is a poor school in which to learn the first principles of Christ's laws in their application to a subject of such vast importance to the church and our country. We must have a higher influence to mould us. If we would sympathize with "those in bonds as bound with them" in a Christ-like manner, we must learn of him the nature of our bondage to sin, and partake of the "liberty wherewith he makes free." Thus shall we learn compassion, not only for those under the bonds of the slave code, but also for those who by it are in a much worse condition. To counteract the evil workings of this system, it is quite as important to apply "the golden rule" in dealing with masters as it is with their servants. Their condition appeals as strongly to our compassion; and upon every Christian principle our hearts will go out towards them with quite as much solicitude. It is through them, mainly, that we can rationally expect to ameliorate the condition of the slave; and, manifestly, it is through them that we can most effectually counteract the pernicious influences of the system in all our social, political, and church relations. If they become interested in Christ's reformatory principles, they must be led by the same kind hand that attends all Christian efforts to take their place at his feet. They must be invited to share in his heavenly blessings, spiritual and holy, and also pointed to the temporal blessings which flow therefrom. They must be made to feel that we are dealing with One whose system of government is so administered as to secure the best interests of all his loyal subjects, both for time and for eternity. None ever gave "the righteousness of his kingdom" the first place in their hearts and lives, that ever found their true interests to suffer as the result. While they must be incited by all the high and holy motives of the gospel to induce obedience to its principles, they must also be pointed to the retribution of an impartial Judge upon the disobedient — of One who "has no respect for persons."

Let us refer to the teachings of the apostles, and see if this was not their manner. Take this exhortation for example: "Masters, give unto your servants that which is just and equal; knowing that ye also have a Master in heaven." (Col. 4: 1.) No one can understand the true meaning of "just and equal," as everywhere interpreted by the apostle, and not admit that this is, virtually, a command to emancipate wherever, on the basis of the golden rule, the slave had a claim to his freedom ; and that, even if the relation continues, it virtually annuls the laws making him property, and places him under the equitable laws of Christ. If this relation is continued under this injunction, the servants are not *held and treated as property*, but according to the equity of Christ's higher law. So when the apostle gives instruction to servants, he points them, also, to this higher law, and says, " Servants, be obedient to them which are your masters according to the flesh, with fear and trembling, in singleness of *your heart, as unto Christ;* not with eye-service, as men-pleasers, but as the servants of Christ, doing the will of God from the heart; with good will doing service, as unto the Lord, and not to men." And, if this is good instruction for servants, it is equally good for masters; for he adds, " And, ye masters, do the same things; knowing that your Master is in heaven, neither is there respect of persons with him."

We see that, according to Christ's laws, the relation is equitable and reciprocal, in which both master and servant are to be governed by the law of love, that binds them mutually to him as their King. Each is pointed to his "Master in heaven," and to the supreme allegiance owed to him and his laws, as their rule of life. Masters had the *power*, under Nero's government, to oppress their servants, and "to doom them to live without knowledge, and without the capacity to call any thing their own;" but they had neither the disposition nor the right to do it under the reign of Christ.

Does any one believe that, if the laws of Christ's kingdom had been thus faithfully applied to this system among us by his professed followers, we should now present to the world the humiliating spectacle which we do? A large section of our country in rebellion and attempted revolution — endeavoring to establish a separate government — adopting the constitution under which we live, after changing the foundations upon which our government rests from liberty and equity to "the Heaven-given right" to oppress and doom an inferior race! As interpreted by one of its highest functionaries, the new government is "founded upon exactly the opposite ideas" which underlie our constitution, and this "Heaven-given right" to enslave is claimed as a great improvement upon the old idea. This official boldly says, "This our new government is the first in the history of the world based upon this great physical, philosophical, and moral truth. This truth has been slow in the process of its development, like all other truths in the various departments of science. It has been so *even amongst us*. Many who hear me, perhaps, can recollect well that this truth was not generally admitted, even within their day. The errors of the past generation still clung to many as late as twenty years ago." *

Yes, professed followers of Jesus! while you have been divided in your counsels between much wrong action and no action at all, the enemy has been busily "sowing tares." A slow growth the new doctrine has had; but it has been making sure progress *downwards*, and we are now reaping the bitter fruit.

The great enemy does not slumber in his efforts to corrupt and subvert righteous principles, and shall we continue to slumber over the unholy working of such corruptions? We plead for no false philanthropy and spurious reform. We know of no gospel principle that requires us to enter upon a mission to incite slaves to insurrection; that shall place in their hands instruments of death, with which they may fight their way to liberty; or that shall create discontent among them, and urge them to abscond. The intermeddling with slaves through the "underground railroad" operations appears to us too much "underground" to have any affinity with Christ's reform. He teaches that slaves be " in subjection to their masters with all fear, not only to the good and gentle, but also to the froward." His is not a reform of force, that is led on and

* Alexander H. Stephens's Speech.

effected by "Sharp's rifles" and the implements of carnal warfare. His weapons of moral warfare "are not carnal, but mighty through God;" and they are mighty in their influence for reform, because they are not carnal.

Government must have its weapons of defence and the means of enforcing its laws; and it is high Christian duty to sustain our government and its laws by repelling insubordination and quelling rebellion, if necessary. Individuals, too, are bound to protect their own lives and those of others from the assassin's deadly knife. But in Christ's kingdom "he that takes the sword" to enforce and promote his principles must expect "to perish with the sword." The efficient instrument in extending Christ's reform is "the sword of the Spirit," wielded in faith and love.

This is our mission. Its limits are defined by no geographical lines. The dominion of Immanuel extends "from sea to sea, and from the rivers to the ends of the earth."

The obligation to our beloved constitutional government is sacred; but our allegiance to the "King of kings" must control it all. Even those who acknowledge no "higher law" than that which makes men "chattels," do at times wish to enforce some of these constitutional obligations by an appeal to Paul's Epistle to Philemon, and bring it directly home to the Christian's conscience. In this we would rejoice. It is well that we may be referred to this source for instruction. Those who are praying, "Thy kingdom come," must earnestly desire to see the time when Christ's principles shall be so brought to bear upon this institution, that they can carry out their constitutional obligations on the principles advocated by Paul in this Epistle.

Let us refer to the principles which he enunciated in returning Onesimus to his master, and see if they do not spring from the same source of divine benevolence that characterized all his missions of love. He says to Philemon, that he would gladly have retained his servant, "but without thy mind would I do nothing; that thy benefit should not be, as it were, of necessity, but willingly. For, perhaps, he therefore departed for a season, that thou shouldst receive him forever; not now as a servant, but above a servant, a brother beloved, specially to me; but how much more unto thee, both in the flesh and in the Lord! If thou, therefore, count me a partner, receive him as myself. If he hath wronged thee, or oweth thee aught, put that on my account." (Phil. 14–18.)

When will the time come in which the same fraternal, benevolent spirit shall pervade the intercourse of Christians in different sections of our land upon this subject? Not while they persistently shut out gospel light, but when they cordially embrace it and apply it. For it is only as our consciences are enlightened by gospel truth that they can be brought to harmonize upon a subject in which error is so artfully intermingled as to corrupt Christian intercourse.

Can any well-instructed conscience object to sending back "fugitives" upon the principles that prompted Paul to return Onesimus? We confess that we wish the whole slave population in the land could be placed in just the position in which Paul's teaching would place them — "not as a servant, but above a servant, a brother beloved." We would that all professed Christians in our land would enter into full sympathy with the apostle. What a blessed change would be produced in our beloved country, if such sentiments pervaded the church in all its borders! How long a time would elapse before every bond would be sundered by the peaceful, voluntary action of those who have the power so to act? "If," says Paul, "thou count me a partner, receive him as myself." This is the spirit, this the manner, of all his instructions to masters. He is always very careful to remind them that "there is no respect of persons with God;" that under his government no enactment of man can discharge them from the law of impartial, disinterested love and righteous equity. Men may frame their slave codes, and by tribunals of their own creation such enormities may be recognized as binding laws. Not so at the judgment seat of Christ! Those who take Christ's laws as their guide, must therefore look at this subject from a higher standpoint than those who are looking at it merely from a financial point of view.

Christ's followers in the free states are often told, "You have nothing to do with this subject, because you are not interested in *slaves as property.*" No interest! Why, they have an interest as much above the mere dollar and cent interest, as heaven is above the earth. They have an interest, in common with others, in the material prosperity of our country; and they love their country for its wise constitutional government, for their freedom under it, and for the numerous blessings it confers. They are willing to sacrifice their own ease and comfort — in short, any thing consistent with their convictions of righteousness — for its preservation; but when the province of a well-instructed Christian conscience is touched, a subject is touched that cannot be estimated by dollars and cents; and those who would sacrifice that conscience in the hope of a temporary gain to material interests must remember that they take upon themselves a very weighty responsibility in thus jeopardizing the highest interests of our country, and imperilling the very existence of our constitutional government, by their rejection of God's methods of securing that government. Has he not firmly established the principles, that "righteousness exalteth a nation," while deliberate, high-handed, and persistent iniquity will not go unpunished? And are not his people the custodians of his principles? Can they see them trampled under foot, and be indifferent? They would be compelled to unlearn all that his word has clearly taught of their beneficial nature and design, before they could become indifferent to the deliberate attempt made to wed the unrighteous system of slavery to those holy principles.

This never can be accomplished, except by shutting out the light. We have seen what has been the result of that policy, as pursued hitherto, and with this gloomy picture staring them in the face, Christ's followers must take warning; and if they awake to their duty in the premises — as we trust in God they will — they will have no occasion to despond. The issue has been distinctly made up — boldly proclaimed. They are not now sailing under false colors. The leaders in the rebellious ranks frankly admit that the prevailing idea of the *framers of our constitution* was " that the enslavement of the African race was in violation of the laws of nature ; that it was wrong in principle, socially, morally, and politically ; and that somehow or other, in the order of Providence, the institution would be evanescent, and pass away."*

* Alexander H. Stephens's Speech.

It is, therefore, with this principle of our fathers and our fathers' God, that they have joined issue, and against which they have arrayed themselves in flagrant rebellion.

Shall we, however, dwell upon this gloomy picture to enkindle sectional animosity? Nothing could be farther from the true spirit of Christ's principles. The evil which is upon us is too distressing to admit of this. We have no time to waste in criminations and recriminations for the wrongs of the past—wrongs in which we fear we are all too deeply involved to allow of any throwing the first stone at the more guilty. With shame we must admit that no subject has been discussed with more acrimony, even in religious conventions and among the ministers of Jesus, than this very subject, which demands the exercise of the utmost Christian love.

This country was dedicated to freedom by our Christian fathers, after extraordinary hardships and trials, such as were calculated to bring out the highest Christian virtues. It was consecrated to the attainment of a much higher end than merely temporal prosperity, although this has been secured in an uncommon degree. Its whole history, however, points it out as destined to bear an important part in extending the reign of Christ. Shall, then, this bitter enemy—evidently a usurper—be permitted without a vigorous, a righteous contest, to blast all of our fondest hopes? No; it will not, it cannot be. The lovers of Christ's righteousness, in all sections and among all classes, must be sought out and united in the conflict.

While God's judgments are upon us for our sins in this connection, let his people take warning, and go in penitence to their Saviour, and of him learn to meet this sin in the true spirit of gospel principles. And going thus, was there ever a subject that could be presented to him with more hope of success? For, when they shall have learned to grapple for the suppression of this system of iniquity, and for peaceful, voluntary emancipation, they will have learned a very important lesson, which will prepare them to meet other gigantic forms of sin, with which they have to contend in the onward progress of Christ's kingdom. We know these heavenly principles are too tame to meet the demands of the religious frenzy too often cultivated amid the clash of arms and the belligerent feelings engendered thereby; yet they are God's armament, and by him rendered "mighty for the pulling down of the strongholds" of sin, by quieting the raging passions and enkindling calm reflection and peaceful dispositions.

We know not how much may be accomplished for the overthrow of slavery by God's judgments now upon us. He may so order his righteous providence, in his retributive justice, as to make speedy work in its overthrow. Undoubtedly, the very war, so wickedly waged against the government, for the extension and perpetuity of slavery, will result in its more speedy destruction. God speed the right! It is one of the peculiar privileges of the Christian that he belongs to a kingdom where the Supreme Ruler has power to make " the wrath of man praise him," and by it advance his kingdom. But his followers are not dealing out *his* judicial retributions *as their rule of life.* They should learn lessons from all, but such lessons as bring them to Immanuel's feet, *to be taught by his laws.* This is their mission.

They have a high and sacred trust committed to them. It is not, however, "to conserve and perpetuate" an institution that "dooms" and curses an inferior race, nor to deal out vengeance towards those who do; but it is theirs to perpetuate and extend a system that carries *blessings to the weak and helpless wherever found.*

In the prosecution of its beneficent mission towards the enslaved, however, *truth must be afforded an open field in which to combat error in an unrestrained manner*, that thus peaceful emancipation may result; or God will accomplish it in his own way by retributive justice; and *woe be to our land, if we further incur the displeasure of Heaven in this direction!*

VIII.

TRUE PRINCIPLES FOR A BROAD CHURCH.

EVERY one who understands the nature of Christ's kingdom, and believes in the final triumph of its principles, is also, of necessity, a believer in Christian progress. All, however, is not Christian progress that claims to be such. Hence there is need of Christian conservatism enough to investigate and discriminate between the spurious and the true.

Many deem the principles which have been laid down in the foregoing pages as essential for the accomplishment of works of righteousness, to be obstacles in the way of progress. They complain that the gate of entrance is too strait, and the way in which alone we can walk with God in newness of life too narrow. They would enlarge Christ's church by widening the platform upon which its members are to stand. They would construct one broad enough in its terms to take in all the different forms of self-constituted righteousness, graduated according to the different standards which each shall erect. This should be their basis of action, and they would avail themselves to a greater or less extent of Christ's assistance as the system of each shall require. Some would even enlarge the platform to such an extent as to embrace the open despisers of Christ's work of redemption, and of Christianity itself, provided only they have used its borrowed light for the cultivation of humanity, while they utterly contemn and reject Christ's true method of culture. This they call Christian liberality; although it would forever confine immortal souls in the narrow prison-house which selfishness has erected, and repudiate and scorn that liberty extended by the blessed Redeemer to every soul which he frees from its bondage to sin, and unites to himself in all the glorious liberty of the children of God. In the face of this fact, a pretentious claim to Christian liberality is put forth in behalf of this scheme,— nay, even to Christian progress,— and its advocates stigmatize from their stand-point Christ's principles of reform, such as have been presented in these pages, as illiberal, narrow, and bigoted. Indeed, we have no doubt they appear in this light to a great multitude; since whether they are regarded as ennobling or contracted depends entirely upon the criterion by which actions are estimated.

The apostle Paul's estimation of his works after his conversion differed very materially from that in which he had previously held them; and the whole of that difference arose from the different standard by which he formed his judgment in the two cases. When he was "going about to establish his own righteousness," and *self* was the centre of his desires and purposes, he felt that his zeal for God, his self-devotion and laborious toil for him, ought to be respected; and he entertained no doubt that it would be received with favor. He regarded the followers of the despised Nazarene as exceedingly narrow and mischievous in their views, and thought that he was doing God great service in his incessant labors to exterminate them from the face of the earth. "But when the commandment came," what a radical change was wrought in all his views and feelings! Was his mind, however, dwarfed and circumscribed by this change? When was it more enlarged? when selfishness and self-love were the centre from which all his motives, purposes, and volitions emanated? or when Christ was enthroned as the supreme object of his affections, and the establishment of his reign became the controlling object of his life? Was it not when he counted every thing which was gain for self as loss to Christ? when his own righteousness was felt to be worthless, and his ruling desire was to be found "in Christ," that he might have all his inclinations, purposes, and affections flow from the new life " in him " ? There can be no question from which stand-point he received the most enlarged conceptions, if Christ is to be the judge. Is there any other being capable of maintaining a counter criterion of judgment? The principles of action which are now formed in us take hold of immortal interests and eternal destinies; and if they are to stand the test of Him " who will judge the world in righteousness," they must rest upon a basis established by him.

Grant that those who are unwilling to submit themselves to " Christ's righteousness " do now succeed in drawing around them a very large company, — of what avail is it? Though the number of those who are walking in " the strait and narrow way " may seem to them comparatively *diminutive*, yet let them know that this illusion will be utterly dissipated when the end is seen. Let none deceive themselves, because hitherto but few relatively have found the way of life with God. The end of this way is destined to be triumphantly glorious, not only in the height of its joys, but in the extent of the dominion obtained. Although in the strength of its principles, as well as in the extent of its domain, Christ's kingdom is yet in its infancy, yet we are not " following cunningly devised fables" when laboring for its establishment. Look at some of the promises in reference to its extension. How bright are their pictures of reform!

"The kingdoms of this world shall become the kingdoms of our Lord and of his Christ." "Ask of me, and I will give thee the heathen for thine inheritance, and the uttermost parts of the earth for thy possession." "I will gather all nations, and tongues and cause them to come and see my glory." "From the rising of the sun even to the going down of the same, my name shall be great among the Gentiles; and in every place shall incense be offered to my name, and a pure offering." "Ethiopia shall stretch forth her hands unto God." "All nations shall call him blessed." "The wilderness and the solitary place shall be glad for them, and the desert shall rejoice and blossom as the rose. It shall blossom abundantly, and rejoice even with joy and singing." "At the name of Jesus every knee shall bow, and every tongue confess that he is Christ, to the glory of God the Father." "The mountain of the Lord's house shall be established in the top of the mountains, and shall be exalted among the hills, and all nations shall flow unto it." "For the earth shall be filled with the knowledge of the glory of the Lord, as the waters cover the sea."

The period is to arrive, when the world in its moral aspect shall present the counterpart of this cheering view; when from every spot upon its surface shall ascend pure offerings unto Jesus in one continual stream of holy obedience to the principles of his kingdom. Painful, indeed, is the contrast between what the world is to be and what it now is! Although great achievements have been made in disseminating the principles of Christ's kingdom since modern missions commenced, and though very much has been accomplished to gladden Christ's people, yet when compared with what remains still to be done, it is but as a beginning — enough to show God's marked favor towards the enterprise, and the great lack of faith and holy obedience to his commands on the part of his followers. God has sealed the enterprise as his own by his great mercies towards it, and now by his providence is continually opening wide fields which invite vastly increased Christian effort.

How is this demand to be met? There is a decided feeling among all classes of Christians that something more effectual than has yet been attempted must be done to meet the pressure of the emergency. Many endeavors have consequently been put forth to supply the acknowledged deficiency; but, prescribe remedies as we may, none can prove efficacious for the accomplishment of such mighty results that does not derive its *power* from the *Divinity* enstamped upon the whole undertaking. We must have the spirit of a living faith, which will unite the soul in closer affinity with God, and a heavenly sympathy which will lead it to seek the glory of God, over all, in and through all, and as the end of all. We must have that grace, "that is at once positive in its attractions to the good, negative in its repulsions of the evil; negative of error, positive of truth; negative of man, positive of God;" which is moved, not by a desire for happiness, but by a love for Jesus — a benevolence that rises above human expedients and policy to achieve its success.

We have before us God's method by which he infuses in man this efficient working power; and man has never been able to improve upon it. We hear much said of the progress in theological science by the aid of human philosophy; but if it is only surface work, — as much of it unquestionably is, making conversion more easy because superficial, — then it becomes a dangerous enemy, instead of a true friend, of Christ's reform. Although similar influences have always been at work, never have they been more adroitly used than in our day. It is our aim, however, rather to discover what true reform is, and the principles by which it may be extended, than to detect its counterfeits. It is our firm belief that the basis of all substantial and true progress is the result of a divine life within, which, in its union with Christ, changes and transforms the most highly cultivated phases of humanity, and in its workings so allies the soul with Christ that all its strength, all its impulses to action, all its emotions, all its ends, aims, and intentions that are righteous, are received from this supply of spiritual life. Is not this, as a motive power, far superior to all natural qualifications?

Every other motive gains or loses power with the changes in man's condition; every other basis shifts with shifting circumstances; every other fountain may be dried up; but let our souls be linked to Jesus in divine life, let devoted, affectionate attachment to him and his principles prompt the unceasing aspiration, "Thy kingdom come," and we shall find that he hath set our feet firmly upon a rock, from which they cannot be moved. (Ps. 40: 2.) From a fount like this, never-failing employment, unceasing support, and unspeakable joy do continually flow. The establishment of such a kingdom is but a single enterprise; yet it is vast and comprehensive in its extent, reaching into the eternal ages. Let our souls commune with it in spirit; let us give our every energy to its establishment, thus laying up for ourselves a treasure that shall never fail. The feeblest mind may comprehend it, love it, and cling to it in the strength vouchsafed by the great Captain of our salvation; and minds of the most enlarged powers must, in common with all others, receive it and pursue it with all the humility and reverence of little children.

The wondrous power which those acquire who concentrate their every thought and energy upon a single object we all know. Illustrations of the absorbing intensity of a *ruling passion* we have all witnessed. A passion for the acquisition of gold, for fame, for learning, for conquest, has wrought wonders — achievements surpassing belief, had they not been actually witnessed. Obstacles, of whatever nature they may be, are entirely disregarded by such devotees; opposition only inflames their passions, quickens their energies, and invigorates their whole system, physical and mental. Now, there is no passion or principle upon earth that can compare in strength, durability, and efficiency with this holy passion for the establishment of the throne of God and the Lamb. (Rev. 22: 3.) It is an increase in this energizing power that is so much needed to give greater efficiency to our missionary and reformatory enterprises. This is the kind of reform which is needed to regulate our fountains of influence in Christ's kingdom. All who would successfully "hold forth the word of life" to a world "alienated from the life of God," must have their inspiration from this source, their energies quickened by this stimulant. The demand of the age is for a *practical Christianity;* and as we look back upon Christianity as it was exhibited in the primitive church, and learn of its moving power for practical reform, we see the need of the same potent influence in our own times.

Would we have the inspiriting faith and holy zeal which actuated the early Christians, our faith and zeal must be kindled, as was theirs, at the altar of God, and ever kept burning and bright. We must go back, and study more thoroughly their impelling springs of action, and learn what it was that fitted them for their bold and aggressive attacks upon Satan's kingdom. We shall find them going forth in their work full of hope and joyful expectation that their labors would be successful. But how was this hope stimulated? Upon what was it founded? We find that, when Jesus had committed the work to his disciples as instruments for the extension of his kingdom on the earth, he left them with the promise of the Spirit as the Divine Agent to enable them to carry it forward. He was to lead them into all truth relative to that kingdom; to enlighten, comfort, purify, and guide in all things pertaining to their work, and to make his truth effectual for the reformation of the world. His principles were to be declared and established throughout the earth. Their eyes now turn upward. All their expectations centre in the *promise of Jesus*. "They were all with one accord in one place;" prayer and supplication thus going up as from one heart to the faithful Promiser. And what earnest supplication! All looked to their just ascended Lord.

Behold, now, that faithful band assembled in that upper room. To them was intrusted the glorious work of reforming the world, bringing it back to God, and placing it under the reign of Jesus. No plans of their own had they; nor could they place any dependence upon their own agency in the mighty work. As yet they had but faint conceptions of the stupendous results which were to follow their labors. Jesus — their adored One, to whom their hearts were knit together in love — had *given them a charge, and a promise of a Divine Agent* who was to be their future guide. Their confidence was in that *promise*. No one can possibly mistake the *source* whence they expected success.

Now, mark the result! In compliance with that gracious promise in which they trusted, the

Spirit descended in answer to their supplications; and herein, and herein alone, is the secret of their efficiency and their success. As we see distinctly marked the source whence their help was to come that success might crown their efforts, so we see the result of the promised Divine Agency as distinctly marked in the change which followed his descent. Thus we trace the fruits of the promised blessing directly to the faithful Promiser, and find the divinity of the Agent enstamped upon the hearts of those that believed. As the fruit of the Spirit's work, we find their hearts united to Jesus in holy benevolence. This was the special and marked result of his work. It made the disciples of Jesus bold in proclaiming the truth; yet their boldness was the boldness of faith guided by love. They were faithful in pointing out to the enemies of Jesus their guilt and danger in thus arraying themselves against God. This guilt was seen and felt; sinners acknowledged their sins, were "pricked in their hearts," and cried out with anxious solicitude, "Men and brethren, what shall we do?" Being directed to Jesus as the source of help, they committed their souls to him, and through the power of the Holy Spirit were transformed from his bitter enemies to his loving friends.

In the divine record of the operation of the

gospel system, thus organized under the reign of the Spirit, we find that at the outset it triumphed in every place. No form of selfishness which Satan could devise could stand before it. It went forth conquering and to conquer. "And all which believed were together, and had all things common, and sold their possessions and goods, and parted them to all men as every man had need." They went every where, preaching the gospel. They felt that they had charge of the bread of life for a famishing world, and they could not but break and dispense it. "The love of Christ constrained them." They judged that "if one died for all, then were all dead;" "dead in trespasses and sins;" and that "if Christ died for all," then they which were "made alive by him should not henceforth live unto themselves, but unto him that died for them." As if his last command were still ringing in their ears, they longed to proclaim the gospel unto every creature. They felt the dignity of their high position in thus being made the almoners for the world, executors of their Saviour's testament, dispensers of his bounty, and guardians of the most sacred trusts in the universe. In the discharge of their high commission death met them at almost every step; persecution, arrayed in its most terrific garb, was placed in their paths; but " none of these things moved them;" they scarcely deigned to notice them, but continued their divine work of dispensing happiness to man, being impelled thereto by a love which was stronger than the fear of death.

Wherever they went they attracted the attention of all classes; for never before had such an exhibition of benevolence been manifested. In all places they worked their way through this violent opposition, and it yielded to their fidelity and surrendered to their doctrines. Yet the whole secret of their triumphant success was their *union with Christ in divine love*. Diversified as they were in intellect, condition, and age, but one feeling swayed them, one subject of emulation absorbed all others — which should do most to extend the reign of divine love. A fire was thus kindled at the altar of God which proved a sure antidote for the selfishness of man. A work was thus commenced which should restore to man that soundness of spiritual condition which was the birthright of the head of the race.

Thus was the gospel first presented; such were the efficient instrumentalities employed by the Redeemer in and for its introduction to man; and by the use of similar means must it progress and increase in power, until complete victory is obtained. It is "the stone cut out of the mountains without hands," which is to be enlarged until it "becomes a great mountain, and fills the whole earth." (Dan. 2 : 45.) For our King "must reign until he hath put all enemies under his feet." (1 Cor. 15 : 25.)

All must admit that theirs was a *practical Christianity*. Nor is it difficult to understand what kind of truth was instrumental in promoting it. With them God's perfections and character, in all the infinitude of his majesty and glory, were the centre and source of all religious truth — from these all practical truth radiated. Starting from this point of departure, we learn the duty of entire consecration to him, the disinterested love of our whole heart for him, the unconditional submission of all our faculties to him, and a willingness that he should do all things for his own glory. God must have this central place in our affections, or we do not begin to learn *practical obedience* to him. If we have any theory or philosophy of obedience which does not unreservedly accord to him this place, it is a spirit of rebellion, however it may be gilded over or adorned.

In God's system, as we have seen, true obedience is the fruit of Christ's work, as Redeemer and Saviour, in which we partake of his righteousness; and as he graciously grants this heavenly gift only when and as we feel our utter destitution, the ruin of man by nature, and the deceitful, corrupt outgoings of the natural heart, are essential truths, which must be deeply felt in order that we may exhibit this practical Christianity. Our moral condition by nature being a spirit of disobedience, — the whole race, from their connection with the first Adam, partaking of it, and possessing a true, holy, and obedient disposition only through the second Adam, the God-man, — the entire work of redemption has a prominent place in the consideration of practical truth. For this purpose, Christ, in all his various offices as Prophet, Priest, and King, is at work in this system of practical Christianity. As man is a rational being, and as such rationally accountable to God for his actions, and as he is conscious of acting freely in his choices and doings, inasmuch as he is moved to act through motives presented to his mind, — all the motives which God has presented must be used, showing the wretched condition of those " out of Christ," and the infinite blessings of those who are sheltered " in him." We have taken a view of some of the more prominent truths at work in practical Christianity; and if our practice is to be such as God will approve, is it possible in any way to build that practice up by disparaging such truths?

God has established a system of revelation for promoting righteousness; and truth, not error, is to build up Christ's kingdom. Those, therefore, who would successfully build for Christ, will be led to " contend earnestly for the faith once delivered to the saints." This they will do, from the character of their new life and its intimate connection with the truth. To its success in the world they cannot be indifferent; and their affectionate interest in its success will induce them to discriminate between truth and error. In their eyes error loses none of its odious features because it may be dressed in a beautiful garb; nor is it any the less hateful from its close proximity to truth. Satan is no more lovely to them when he is disguised as " an angel of light," than when he appears in his true character. A false and vitiated view of Christ's salvation, by whatever name called, is the most mischievous of all the elements of evil. The religion of the Bible is the bread of heaven, and the water of life. Would he be an enemy who should poison the bread and water upon which we depend for subsistence? Much more should he be regarded as a foe who perverts the gospel, and makes a savor unto death of what was intended to be a savor of life unto life.

The contest between the kingdom of Christ and the kingdom of Satan being a conflict between principles as deeply seated as the moving springs of action, it resolves itself into a struggle whether the Redeemer shall succeed in his glorious work of reëstablishing in the soul the government of *holy benevolence*, or whether man shall continue in his rebellion, and maintain his own independence, governed by his own ruling self-love.

As the entire economy of salvation is constructed upon the principle of restoring to the soul that holy love which was lost in the fall of man, the endeavor to rescue it brings into antagonism, and tests, the relative strength of this holy benevolence and the fallen self-love of the carnal mind — the darling principle of heaven and the controlling principle of all revolt and ruin. It is this view of the nature of the conflict which binds the good soldier of the cross to the Captain of his salvation. Every victory won not only strengthens those spiritual bands that unite to him, but also renders more endearing the precious principles of his kingdom, which find their outgoings in renewed activities to extend and establish them in the world. They cannot be put " under a bushel," but must be announced abroad, and their claims urged in the name and with all the authority of their Divine Author. Their antagonism to the spirit of the world necessarily renders the work aggressive, and aggressive to such a degree that in its operation it *unites to the Beloved*, because the reform is too radical for the power of man to accomplish. As we battle for victory over sin in ourselves, and in the world, we gain renewed strength proportioned to the aggressions which we make, and we feel more keenly our own weakness for the conflict as we gain a clearer insight into the holy nature of the work. This again prepares the way for a still richer experience of what we can do " through Christ who strengthens us." At each advancing step we are drinking more deeply from this inexhaustible Fountain of spiritual life.

While these are the efficient principles, and this the experience, of " the good soldier of Jesus Christ," he has to encounter those fighting under the same banner as himself who would enlist soldiers of the cross upon different principles; and yet so skilfully do they proceed in their undertaking that it not infrequently would seem as if they were trained in it as a science. They encourage the recruits to go forth to the conflict against sin armed with the power they have inherent in themselves. They inscribe " love " upon their banners, and talk truthfully of its potent power; but they do not plead for *supernatural* love. They say " love in man [in man by nature] is the same in kind as love in God;" that all the change needed is, that it be put forth upon right objects; that there is no deeper work than can be accomplished by the determined choice of man in the exercise of the power of his own free will. They would make use of God's means of grace for cultivating the natural, rather than to trust in Jesus to impart life divine and supernatural.

There is a great difference between enlisting those who are willing to declare themselves for Christ, and to enter upon a self-righteous work, and enlisting those who have their names written in "the Lamb's book of life" by the Holy Spirit. There are two prominent modes of enlisting: the one, by converting the principles of the gospel into conformity with the views and tastes of the carnal mind, and the other, by converting the carnal mind into conformity with the truth by a spiritual renewal of the heart. The former would construct a system of salvation adapted to the supreme self-love of man; the latter would bring man by a supernatural change to a supreme love of God.

We believe that the gist of the practical difference between these reformatory principles is to be found in the views entertained of that love which is "the fulfilling of the law." All are ready to unite in encomiums upon the benevolent characteristics of the gospel; and it is much more pleasant to fallen humanity to descant upon the beauties of Christ's Sermon on the

Mount than to "pluck out the right eye" in order to render obedience to its precepts. It is much more congenial to the rebellious spirit in man to bring down God's standard of righteousness to his own conceptions of right doing than to yield submissively to his requirements. Most of those who bear the Christian name are ready to applaud the bold, uncompromising, and aggressive labors of the primitive Christians and the true reformers of every age; but all do not as readily acquiesce in the uncompromising nature of their conversion to God. Yet this it was that made them bold, uncompromising, and aggressive in their practical Christianity. How many are ready to extol the uncompromising nature of the religion of our Puritan fathers, who yet labor to compromise and modify the very doctrines which formed the life-blood of that religion. Many claim to have sympathy with, and to be believers in, the "Theology of New England," as taught by Edwards and the divines of his day, who yet adopt principles that subvert the very foundation of their theological system.

We can see what was claimed to be the practical working-power of Edwards's system of theology by looking at its results, as set forth in his treatise on the "Religious Affections." It is in "the affections," according to his teaching, "that true religion centres." We are most distinctly told that holy affection is the essence of all true religion, and that its great value and *real efficacy* consist in its being a *special gift of God*, wrought in the soul by the power of the Holy Spirit. We refer to that treatise in this connection, because we know of no other discrimination of the affections that so perfectly corresponds with the teachings of the Bible, or which sets forth the actuating power of holy affections so forcibly; and it is moreover a standard work in our churches.

He says, (Part III,) "Regenerate persons are called spiritual, because of the indwelling and holy influences of the Spirit of God in them. . . . The Spirit of God is given to the true saints, to dwell *in them* as his proper, lasting abode, and to influence their hearts as a principle of new nature, or as a divine, supernatural spring of life and action. . . . He is represented as being so united to the faculties of the soul that he becomes there a principle or spring of new nature and life. . . . The Spirit of God, dwelling as a vital principle in their souls, there produces those effects wherein he exerts and communicates himself in his own proper nature, which is holiness; and that holiness is of the same nature with the divine holiness, as much as it is possible for that holiness to be which is infinitely less in degree."

He further shows how this new principle of life within becomes vastly superior as a moving power, by contrasting it with the working of the minds of natural men. "The Spirit of God never influences the minds of natural men after this manner. Though he may influence them in many ways, yet he never in any of his influences communicates himself to them in his own proper nature. Indeed, he never acts disagreeably to his nature, either in the minds of saints or sinners. But the Spirit of God may act on man agreeably to his own nature, and not exert his *proper nature in the acts* and exercises of their minds."

He contends, as another has said, "that the Spirit does exert his proper nature in the acts and exercises of those united to Christ in holiness. He is so united to the faculties of the regenerate soul as to be active to exert his proper nature in its acts. He acts *in them*. He is active in their activity. But it is not so with respect to natural men. He does not act *in* their minds; he acts *on* their minds as an external agent, presenting ideas of duty, of guilt, of danger, and thus producing in them conviction, alarm, and anxiety, of which the natural man is capable on natural principles. But he does not act *in* the activity of their minds so as to communicate his own moral attribute of holiness to their action," as he does in those who are "born of the Spirit." "The true saints only," he says again, "have that which is spiritual; others have nothing which is divine, in the sense that has been spoken of. They not only have not these communications of the Spirit of God in so high a degree as the saints, but have nothing of that *nature or kind*. . . . From these things it is evident that those gracious influences which the saints are subjects of, and the effects of God's Spirit which they experience, are entirely above nature, altogether of a different kind from any thing that men find within themselves by nature, or only in the exercises of natural principles; and are things which no *improvement* of those qualifications or principles that are natural, no advancing or exalting them to higher degrees, and no kind of composition of them, will ever bring men to; because they not only differ from what is natural, and from every thing that natural men experience, in *degree and circumstances*, but also in *kind*, and are of a nature vastly more excellent. And that is what I mean when I say that gracious affections are from those influences that are supernatural."

According to his reasoning, it is not only a supernatural influence which is at work, but it so works as to produce a supernatural affection towards God. This new spiritual life which the Spirit imparts to the soul at the new birth he styles " a new spiritual sense." He says, " In those gracious exercises and affections which are *wrought in the minds of the saints* through the saving influence of the Spirit of God, there is a new inward perception or sensation of their minds, entirely different in its nature and kind from any thing that ever their minds were the subjects of before they were sanctified. . . . There is some new sensation or perception of the mind, which is entirely of a new sort, and which could be produced by no exalting, varying, or compounding of that kind of perceptions or sensations which the mind had before. . . . And here is, as it were, a new spiritual sense that the mind has, or a principle of a new kind of perception or spiritual sensation, which is in its whole nature different from any former kind of sensations of the mind, as tasting is diverse from any of the other senses." The Spirit, working " in the mind of natural men, only moves, impresses, assists, improves, or in some way acts upon natural principles, but gives no *new* spiritual principle. . . . In those awakenings and convictions that natural men have, God only assists conscience, which is a natural principle, to do that work in further degree which it naturally does. Conscience naturally gives men an apprehension of right and wrong, and a retribution. The Spirit of God assists men's consciences to do this in a greater degree — helps conscience against the stupefying influence of worldly objects and their lusts. And so, many other ways might be mentioned, wherein the Spirit acts upon, assists, and moves natural principles; but, after all, it is no more than nature moved, acted, and improved."

He thus discriminates closely between the mere spiritual improvement of natural faculties and the new, gracious quality which Christ imparts to those united to him. In his discriminations he magnifies Christ's spiritual reform. He speaks of the transforming nature of gracious affections as a " new spiritual understanding, in which the soul has the excellency and glory of divine things *discovered to it*." " The saints have a spiritual perception of God and holiness discovered to them that natural men know nothing of." And these " spiritual discoveries are so transforming, that they not only make an alteration of the present exercise, sensations, and frame of the soul, but such power and efficacy have they, that they make an alteration in the very nature of the soul." " Such power as this is properly divine power, and is peculiar to the Spirit of the Lord. Other power may make a great alteration in men's present frames and feelings; but it is the power of a Creator only that can change the nature, or give a new nature; and no discoveries or illuminatives but those that are divine and supernatural will have this supernatural effect."

He was thus led to distinguish between the saving experience of holy affections and those numerous fair shows and specious appearances by which they are counterfeited. As he distinguished the true, gracious affections of the new spiritual nature from the religious emotions of the natural heart, so he was led to discriminate between the ability which man has by nature from his possessing the complete faculties of a moral agent, and his moral inability, in consequence of his indisposition to use them righteously; the former rendering us accountable, the latter making us guilty and entirely dependent on Christ. The change wrought he every where treats as a moral change, and yet as a work which it is beyond the natural powers to accomplish. The nature of conversion itself led him to dwell upon *man's inability* in the premises.

Although "the Spirit communicates his own proper nature in regeneration," he explains that "it is not a new faculty of understanding imparted," but "a new foundation laid in the nature of the soul for a new kind of exercises of the same faculty of understanding." Yet his acute and penetrating mind could not discover any *philosophical* objections to this view of Christ's work; but he demonstrated that all was carried on in perfect harmony with the laws of the mind.

According to his discrimination, " a new kind of affection " is implanted in the soul at the time of the great change; and every one that thus "loveth is born of God," and has a new spiritual perception of God and holiness. From this spiritual change their choices now emanate, the moving spring of action is transformed, and its working is from " a new spiritual nature," inwrought by the power of the Holy Spirit, who thus communicates his own proper nature. It is not the act of a merely human mind in the exercise of its natural powers, but the act of a mind to which the Holy Spirit had so communicated himself in the new life within as to exert his own proper nature. And hence its wonderful efficiency as a working power. In this age, when calls for increased religious activities are so numerous, do we not need the same kind of discrimination as we have quoted ? We plead for this in this connection, not mainly to promote moods and frames of mind for our own enjoyment, but as an *efficient incentive for benevolent activities*. Vastly important as it is that our religious exercises should be such as to furnish good evidence of a preparation for heaven, yet this object is best secured when we are righteously laboring to extend *Christ's kingdom on earth*. It is exceedingly important to love the truth because of the beauty and sweetness of its moral excellence ; yet this state of mind is not maintained in a healthy and vigorous state, except as we are thereby effectually *united to Jesus in supernatural benevolence*. Its true nature and working were seen as manifested under the preaching of the word on the day of Pentecost. When the Holy Spirit had communicated himself in his *own proper nature* in uniting those early believers to Christ, the new disposition thus received was in its outgoing in striking contrast with the reigning affections of the natural heart.

It is recorded of them, that " all that believed were together, and had all things common, and sold their possessions and goods, and parted them to all men as every man had need." This, however, was not the working of the mere natural mind brought to bear upon the subject of benevolence. On the contrary, they seem to have had no true conception of such a state of mind until they had received it as a special gift, by virtue of their union with Christ. They had thought of their sins and their wretched condition as sinners, and of

Christ as their only Deliverer. These thoughts had *absorbed* their minds, and in believing in him this change came; and when it had come, this benevolent conduct was but its spontaneous outgoing. It was the prompting spirit in their bold and aggressive movements. "Being filled with the Holy Ghost, they spoke the word of God with boldness;" and "they went every where, preaching the word." Now, as then, all hope for *progress* in true reform *centres in Jesus*. From this fountain of supernatural benevolence we must continue to draw for its extension until "the people shall be all righteous," and gospel principles shall so permeate society that the most common affairs of life shall be conducted from a controlling love towards God; till there shall be " upon the bells of the horses, 'Holiness to the Lord,'" and all shall thus know and serve him, "from the least to the greatest."

Many laborers for Christ seem to entertain the opinion that, since the world has advanced in civilization, in culture, in general knowledge, and in refinement, we do not need, in modern times, such manifestations of *divine power for reform* as were requisite in the days of the apostles.

Human nature, however, still remains the same in its disposition towards God. It is just as inimical to the Spirit now as it was in those days. Satan is no less the Christian's adversary; he is no less malignant, artful, and assiduous in compassing his devices; nor have ungodly men abated aught of their opposition to Christ and his holy doctrines. Time has changed the *forms* only in which this hostility is manifested; these being adapted to the present condition of society in its advanced state of civilization.

We as much need help divine to meet the shifting devices of Satan when developed in the most highly cultivated form of human nature, as in its rudest and most barbarous state; and much is to be learned by the followers of Christ upon this subject before they can cope successfully with the many *changing phases of man's religion*. Much rubbish in doctrine and practice must be cleared away in the onward progress of Christ's kingdom. Practices which now greatly mar and clog the working of divine benevolence, must be reformed, and the standard of benevolent activities greatly elevated, if we expect Christ's principles to triumph. We are not to conceive of the millennium as something prepared in heaven, to be let down upon us from the abodes of the blessed at a specified time, or as something to be brought about by the destruction of the wicked. On the contrary, it is to be regarded as but the perfecting and extending of precisely those moral principles which are now more or less actively at work in society. It will, doubtless, be aided by retribution upon the wicked, and greatly hastened by the ordering of God's providence; but it is the moral phase of its warfare, with which the Christian reformer has mainly to do, and in this view we are impelled to the conclusion, that our Christian principles and activities must take the same supernatural hold of God as did the early reformers, and true reformers of every age, or our hopes for final triumph are all visionary.

We have only to glance at the events now transpiring in our own Christian land to be convinced of the necessity of applying these principles to every-day life. How often are our hearts pained by the recital of the barbarities, devastation, and death that attend the civil war now in progress among us! As our hearts sicken at these constantly recurring details, we turn away from them to refresh ourselves with some cheering ray of light from "the Prince of Peace." Has he not a remedy? Yes: while we mourn over these destructive scenes, we are invited to solace our minds with some of the prophetic descriptions which accompany the glorious triumph of his pacific principles. Take for instance the following: "They shall beat their swords into ploughshares, and their spears into pruning-hooks; nation shall not lift up sword against nation, neither shall they learn war any more."

The disciple of Jesus knows that this is no fancy sketch of a vivid imagination, however foreign to this blissful picture may be the present condition of our sin-stricken world. He firmly trusts in it, as destined to become a practical reality. And why should he not? He knows that such a result is but the legitimate fruit of the righteous disposition received from union with Christ. He knows that true peace with God brings with it peace towards man; and that men will be disposed to learn war no more, in proportion as they learn of Him who is "meek and lowly in heart."

If this be the true nature of Christ's work, why should such a striking contrast be presented to it in this Christian land? We know very well that a Christian community, however peaceably disposed, may not always be able to live at peace with others, until Christ's principles have wrought a more thorough work in the world. The apostle says, "If it be possible, as much as lieth in you, live peaceably with all men;" thus implying clearly that it might not always be *possible* to do it. Demands are at times made, which, upon Christian principles, it is not right to grant. These must be contested. Our personal rights we may yield for the sake of peace; but duty to others may compel us to contest the strength of those who make unrighteous demands.

In our land, however, — where we have so large an army enlisted, professedly, under the banner of "the Prince of Peace," — which, as a body, has taken the front rank among his followers in the endeavor to unfurl his standard among every nation under heaven; in a land, which, as we have seemed to suppose, is in advance of all others in "Christian progress," it was, surely, but a reasonable expectation to entertain, that society would have been moulded in accordance with his principles, sufficiently, at least, to have prevented the terrible calamity which is upon us. We cannot look upon the sad spectacle without the deep conviction that the church is very far from its true position, and that much of our boasted progress has been in the wrong direction; that the church has been assimilating itself to the world, instead of assimilating the world to itself; and that we have great reasons to take new lessons from our glorious Leader before we can be prepared to fight successfully his moral battles. As the sacrifice of life and treasure, now rendered inevitable, is teaching us the value of our government, it becomes us to place a higher value on those peaceful moral influences which are mighty in its support.

If we estimate the immense sacrifice of treasure and of valuable time necessary for the organization and maintenance of our vast army, the great amount of suffering endured, the general prostration of business, the terrible loss of life, the anguish and pain of families made desolate thereby, and compare all this with what would be the condition of affairs under a government administered upon the principles of Christ's kingdom, whose subjects are actuated and controlled by the benign influence of those principles,—what a forcible contrast is presented!

The superior excellence of Christ's principles, rightly applied, consists in their *preventing* rebellion, by making all loyal subjects of a *righteous government*. When armed rebellion sets government at defiance, it then becomes a high Christian duty to sustain that government, and in every possible way to promote union and determination, that loyal men may be encouraged to put down that rebellion, at whatever cost. For civil government by God's appointment is "for the punishment of evil-doers and for the praise of them that do well." If its power is set at defiance, it must show that it "beareth not the sword in vain."

We have but to notice the origin of this war-spirit, if we would comprehend the necessity of applying more effectually the heavenly antidote.

"From whence come wars and fightings among you?" "From those lusts which war in your members;" which, as we have seen, Christ's reform is alone effectual to meet. Is it not evident, then, that this must be more faithfully applied, so as to mould society according to his principles, before the inventive genius now upon the rack to devise new and formidable engines of death, by which to accomplish the greatest destruction in the shortest space of time, shall be turned with all its energy to the construction of useful implements wherewith to improve and bless mankind?

We have had rich foretastes of the blessings attending peaceful relations, such as no other nation has ever enjoyed; but in our prosperity, as is man's wont, we have forgotten the Giver — have become self-confident, self-reliant, and boastful; and it especially becomes us to meet the issues now presented to us as faithful soldiers of the cross. Let us now gather around the standard of the cross, and renew our oaths of allegiance, and pledge renewed fidelity to Christ's principles.

We admire the courage and patient endurance of sufferings manifested by those who face the cannon's mouth upon the battle field; but how much more highly should we prize the courage that can face popular error, — gilded over —

shielded with its masked batteries, — and wield against it the power of truth and love!

Rebels in arms against our government cannot be "let alone," though millions of money and thousands of lives have to be sacrificed in defending that government. The united voices of good and loyal subjects bear testimony in word and deed that our government is worthy the sacrifice. And shall we see the government of Immanuel menaced in its stronghold, its vital principles trampled under foot, and not wage a determined conflict against it? On every hand we see the ravages of the enemy spreading desolation and misery in society, and shall we not make an "onward movement" for the rescue? Are we acting the part of true and loyal subjects of that government if we do not gird on the divine armor and go forth to meet the foe at every point of attack?

The great enemy employs many ways for the demoralization of society, and for the accomplishment of his destructive purposes. But, in whatever forms corrupt nature manifests itself, and however malignant its working, we find for it a sure antidote in the fountain opened in "Christ crucified;" and it is vain to seek other remedies less radical and efficient.

If, for example, we look at the enormous evil of Intemperance, we shall find in the principles of the Great Reformer *the only sure and efficient agency for a permanent reform.*

In those principles the Temperance reformation, so happily initiated in our country, had its origin; and to them we must look for its efficient support. The work is too extensive in its nature, and conflicts with too many antagonistic elements with which sinful man is involved, to be successfully carried out without such aid. It is true that total abstinence from intoxicating liquor is demonstrated to be for the well-being of man — that in health he is only injured by its common use; yet we also have the painful demonstration that it is exceedingly difficult to induce society to practically apply these demonstrable truths. How often do families mourn over the fall of a beloved member, who, but for intoxicating drink, would be a comfort and a support! How many persons there are, upon whom total abstinence could be urged, on every principle of natural affection and interest! but how often are these precious influences used in vain! What powerful persuasives are not infrequently brought to bear upon a beloved one, with all the tender love of a devoted wife or mother, whose fond hopes, for a time elated, are only to receive keener anguish by his deeper degradation!

The Christian parent is borne down with grief

by the degrading intemperance of a beloved son, and finding one means after another to fail, is forced to witness the effects of a Satanic, seductive influence which is insidiously working his ruin. With the heart-rending spectacle before him he is led to exclaim, in anguish of soul, "Is there no hope?" He finds that good resolutions are but as the spider's web, and every influence seems powerless before depraved appetite and the fiendish influences used to inflame it. In such circumstances, is there not some effective source open, which is all-powerful to save? Yes, Christian disciple! You are united by birth to One whose relationship, more endeared than that which nature gives, should inspire hope and confidence. You know of his boundless mercy in redeeming work, for you have tasted its saving efficacy. Is not compassion of such magnitude to be trusted? Revert again to the characteristics of his earthly mission, as he "went about doing good." Was not mercy shown to those whom "Satan had bound" in body as well as soul? Is not the same mercy available now?

Associations, combined pledges, and natural sympathies have, indeed, a great power. When to these is added the strong arm of the civil law, we have a powerful agency, preventive as well as reformatory. But, unless to these is superadded a union with the Divine Reformer, we never can cope with triumphant success with the allied forces of the great enemy. Our "moral suasion" must be based upon a divine union with him more potent than merely natural principles or sympathies, or it can never vanquish this powerful foe. All associations and combinations which virtually repudiate this great truth will, in the end, prove a snare and stumbling-block to Christ's true reformers.

We would not deny that much may be done for the good of man in promoting temperance, without taking this high ground. Much, in truth, has been done for his elevation and happiness on other principles. This, however, should not induce Christ's reformers to abandon the elevated position to which his principles would lead them.

Temperance is one of the fruits of the Spirit, and it must have a prominent place in the holy training to which they are to subject themselves in order to be fitted for the Master's service and glory. They need all the holy privileges which are opened to them by virtue of their union with him. Unquestionably, they have much to learn from his spiritual training, before they come up fully to the precept, "Whether ye eat or drink, or whatever ye do, do all to the glory of God." As they drink at this spiritual fountain, they will be better prepared to extend their sympathy and compassion to those who are under the debasing influence of a depraved appetite. They, surely, will not be less sympathetic towards those degraded by vice on account of their holy sympathy with Jesus.

Natural sympathy and compassion have great temporary value; but, after all, reformatory measures based upon them can never reach the lower strata of vice with any hope of effecting a thorough and permanent change. No: in every point of view, the true reformer is pointed to a union in sympathy and compassion with the Atoning Sacrifice. Cut off from every other ground of hope, he rests upon this with a purer faith and an unfailing trust. It links to One, who has control of all agencies, both natural and supernatural, and *he works by them all.*

As from this Fountain flows a benevolence stronger than nature can give, it will in its outgoings secure the necessary funds for all kinds of aggressive work. Bound, as his people are, to their Redeemer in holy affection, they will not suffer his cause to languish for the want of sufficient means to sustain missionary operations.

But, in our present emergency, does it not become us to inquire whether his principles of action are properly regarded in this respect? Do not the means employed oftentimes to procure funds show a great lack of confidence in these principles? Why should appeals to this end be based upon natural and worldly principles, instead of upon those established by our glorious Leader? We cannot go into the subject in detail; but is it not evident that means are too much adapted to suit the tastes of the world in order to secure their approbation and funds?

Many ways of this nature are devised, which tend to secularize and degrade Christian benevolence. As all our hope for prosperity is in God, he should not be the last being upon whom reliance should be placed in carrying forward the work which he has given us to do. With all the evidence before us of the sufferings of our Redeemer to procure for us supernatural benevolence, we may be sure that this is to be the controlling and efficient agency in carrying forward his work. He loves his principles too well, and places too high a value upon the sanctification of his people by them, to commit his cause to other agencies.

Let us, then, be content to be shut up in "the strait and narrow way," never allured by any of the blandishments thrown around the "broad platforms" of man's devising. Although they make *liberal* pretensions, yet, they all conduct to the *narrow prison;* while the "narrow way" will lead us on to victory over sin, and introduce us to a company "as the sands upon the sea shore innumerable."

www.ingramcontent.com/pod-product-compliance
Lightning Source LLC
Chambersburg PA
CBHW021727220426
43662CB00008B/735